# THE HAND OF A STRANGER

# The
# Hand of a Stranger

*(Journal D'un Inconnu)*

JEAN COCTEAU

*Authorised Translation by*
ALEC BROWN

*Essay Index Reprint Series*

 BOOKS FOR LIBRARIES PRESS
FREEPORT, NEW YORK

STANDARD BOOK NUMBER:

8369-1401-5


LIBRARY OF CONGRESS CATALOG CARD NUMBER:

79-99626


PRINTED IN THE UNITED STATES OF AMERICA

# EPIGRAPH:

*We who know what this gesture draws*
*Abandon the dance and the drinkers*
*of wine . . .*

Opera

# TRANSLATOR'S FOREWORD

My dear Author,

I have, you see, not been entirely discouraged by your *"obstacle infranchissable des équivalences"*, though there were moments in one chapter when, battling with too many distants, I craved distance. But I was encouraged in my efforts to render your thought so that not only those who already know would read it, yet not failing to introduce sufficient obstacles to comprehension to have it comprehended, by my own preoccupation (much more indolent of course, than yours) since I was fourteen with that wild-goose chase of the galaxies without and the galaxies within with which as the first world war was beginning one of the world's periodic fits of hysterics I crazed my own mathematics mastcr. Later, past's coitus with future tantalised me under the same Balkan sun and the same hyperlucidity of air as yourself. The sybils whispered to you on the Ionian Sea and Homer spoke to me with Montenegrin *gusla*. But you have written about it and I have not, which was a good passport for translating you. A fascinating task, especially when so many of your potential readers on this side of the Channel apparently think so painstaking a glazier as you are writes paradoxes for the sake of paradox. Their illusion however, does not only come from the deliberate handstands by which, eternal optimist, you hope to provoke the glimmerings of unorthodoxy of thought in an age of servile minds. It also comes from the deceptive likenesses of your French and our English, such close cousins* that English understanding of French writing is often clouded, and of course vice versa. Which is where I come in. To sort

---

* *After all, when the Duke of Orleans spent quarter of a century in English captivity, he could still speak his own language here to all educated men!*

it out. Or try to. Not, I hope, introducing too much order, defeating your devices or on the other hand shocking you by apparently too outrageous departures from the straight path. The words, poor dears, are not to blame in themselves, but because they are crystallisations of generations of ever more diverse habits. (Many Frenchmen still think for themselves, few Englishmen). Take merely the chapter on friendship, where in your tongue *amitié* and *camaraderie* are words of equal rank, denoting two different levels of being, of different rank. In English, of like rank, we have only friend and friendship and thereby open one of our many doors to confused thought. For we have a startling split between the astounding precision of the mechanics of our language, greater than that of French (at least, when used by an educated Englishman, Scotsman, Welshman, or Irishman, but not alas, by alleged cousins oversea), and its vocabulary, so much more imprecise than yours. A whole book could be written on the connotations and associations of such a word as *comrade* in various tongues. Compare the dull, rather unemotional, intimacy of hard toil of the Russians' *tovarishch* ("fellow burden-bearer"), with the simple intimacy of the Yugoslavs' *drug*—which is nothing less than English *mate*, the "other one", the "friend" (as among English Quakers). Yet to render *comrade* in this translation I cannot use the word *mate*, let alone more special terms like the *brother* of printers and some religious sects. *Mate*, for instance, is either specifically a word of the man who labours with his hands or, in its derivatives, (*matey* and *matiness*), with leisured-class sneer assumes a narrow, somewhat pejorative sense. But equally I cannot use the obvious *comrade* because this has been tainted first by memories of the solidarity of jackbooted conquerors (Ich hatte einen Kamerade), then by the puerilities of partyliners as ignorant as they are infantile, with their assumprion that every *gopak* is the creation of Stalin's ant-heapers. And by a perversity both fascinating and frightening our educated folk confuse our thought still further by calling the friends

who are bad (or merely flimsy) "good" while, as if to register
the lamentable fact that as we all become children of totalitarian ways (or of public schools which are not public or of
the other schools which *are* public but try to be non-public
public schools), we confuse and debase our vocabulary still
further by using the potentially precious word *friend* (or
*friendship*), for temporary or experimental sentimental loves
(amourettes) between the sexes or within one sex alone (the
female), while we constrict *comradeship* by peculiarly Spartan,
almost para-military, rigours. It is to blaze a safe trail
through such tangled undergrowth that time and again
I may seem to you to hare off verbally right or left. But then,
have you not pronounced my absolution in advance, with
your true words: "Let us beware of a translation of one of our
works if it looks true to us because it resembles it." So thank
you, and *au revoir*, or *au relire*—you need not reply*.

ALEC BROWN

Tarrant Gunville,
May 30th, 1956.

---

* *Unless you still hold (see p.* 106) *that "nothing dogs me but professional
conscience".*

# DEDICATORY LETTER

My dear René Bertrand,

I was ignorant of you, as one is of the wings of the universe which are your study.

You became my friend after having listened to the radio. I had said: *Time is a phenomenon of perspective.* There you have a case of a grain of seed broadcast blind falling on good soil.

I have written the following notes with my mind on you, on the pessimism of your book *l'Univers cette Unité*, optimistic pessimism, because though you studied our poor work you sprayed your vines with bluestone.

\*       \*       \*

Let me now remind you of that recent business about Einstein which pleased you so much and was reported in the American press.

The University of Philadelphia got a letter from a man of science who announced his discovery of a serious error in Einstein's latest calculations. The letter was sent to Einstein. Einstein declared that the man of science was genuine and if there was a man capable of faulting him, it should be done publicly.

So professors and pressmen were invited to the university. They met in the big lecture hall. There was a blackboard on the platform. And for four hours the man of science covered that blackboard with incomprehensible symbols. At last, pointing to one of these, he said: "That is the error."

Einstein mounted the platform, gazed lengthily at the incriminated symbol, sponged it off, took the chalk and wrote something else in its place.

The challenger then hid his face in his hands, uttered a strange, hoarse cry and rushed out of the hall.

When Einstein was asked to explain this scene, he replied that it would need several years of study for anybody to understand.

Alone on the platform, the blackboard reared its Mona Lisa features. What am I saying, I mean: its terrible abstract blackboard smile.

\*     \*     \*

If either of us were to fault the other, you would be the challenger and I should take to my heels at top speed. But I am not going to put you under the obligation to inflict that humiliation on me.

It remains nevertheless true that the bonds between us are such that I have no more hope in the success of my notes than you have in the success of your books. It is but to express certain truths. They disturb people's comfort. They threaten by force to raise the wing under which man hides his head. An attitude which would have been valid, had he not gone too far and were it not too late to hide one's head after having so often said: "Frighten me!" For that matter, truth has changing features which man can gaze upon without fear because he does not recognise them.

Please accept this dedication as the simple homage of a man invisible to his colleague.

JEAN COCTEAU

Saint-Jean-Cap-Ferrat
February, 1952.

# PRELUDIUM

It is not my pretension to erect a factory of the invisible, but to follow the example of the handicraftsman in matters which demand more culture than I possess,

I intend to set up my little bench at my door and working by hand try to understand on what wisdom bases its industry.

Having neither the tools nor the precepts which might ease such studies, I have to reduce myself to re-bottoming a chair on which the soul rather than the body sits.

I have often felt such pleasure at watching the little trades of the street that I may succeed in satisfying those who take the same pleasure as I do in that sort of scene and such goods.

A man of science told me one day that one had more contact with the mystery if one was not too bundled up in doctrine, more luck if one tossed one's coin onto the figures haphazard, instead of doubling one's stake, that science put the brake on itself by continually re-counting its legs and that a little truancy might get us on to the right road, that one had seen staghounds lose the scent, whereas the nose of a rocket fell on the spot. In short, a thousand nice things in which I look for an excuse for my own ignorance and permission to rebottom my chair.

It was by playing the fiddle badly that Ingres gave us a formula so apt that one wonders what other was used before we had it.

*Several strings to his bow* is not used in the same way. And if Leonardo had been after Ingres, no doubt it would have been said that, being a virtuoso, he played on several fiddles.

I possess neither telescopes nor microscopes. Merely a certain knack at splicing and at choosing my withies.

What I lay claim to is the right to spiritual craftsmanship. Craftsmanship is no longer in favour in our age of big industry.

But it is representative of that singularity which the towering waves of the plural so menace.

P.S. In the country I have noticed, and Montaigne explains it better than I do, how the imagination gets out of control, blindly excited, unless fixed on some definite thing. This day-book or ledger, chapter by chapter, is merely the discipline by which a mind on holiday, suddenly afraid of getting lost by leisure, tries to reconcentrate its thought.

# On Being Invisible

All-capable. The sudden thought that
masterpieces may be merely alibis.

*Essay of Indirect Criticism*

I RATHER believe invisibility to be the essential of style.
Once noticeable, style is no longer. Being the essence of
style, poetry should be invisible. But you will ask me what
use if so it would be. No use. Who perceive it? Nobody. But
that is all no let to its being a mortal threat to false shame,
despite all its exhibitionism affecting even the blind. To
poetry the expression of a personal ethic suffices. Subsequently
such private morality takes on its own being—entitled works
of art, entities, insistent on living their own life, though
becoming the excuse for a thousand misapprehensions
labelled fame.

What makes fame ridiculous is the fact that it is the result of
herd-passions. An accident gathers its little crowd, the crowd
tell each other about it, inventing details and mulling it over
till its nature is completely changed.

Beauty is always the result of an accident, of a brusque
passage from established modes to new modes—which will in
turn be adopted. It disorientates us, disconnects, even dis-
mays. But once the new mode is established, what was
accidental ceases to be so. It becomes classical, then loses its
power to shock. Thus a work of art is never understood,
merely accepted. I think it was Delacroix who said it: "We
are never understood, we are accepted." Matisse was always
repeating these words. The real witnesses of the accident
move on. They are really moved—and unable to tell exactly
what happened. Evidence about it is given by those who
were not present. By this alone, seizing on a fortuitous pretext

to make their little mark, they give expression to their own non-wisdom. Behind them, on the road, the accident itself remains, a blood-bespattered thing, postures petrified. It is now desperately alone, the prey of he said—she said—it is said—and police reports.

\*     \*     \*

All this chit-chat and these reports are inexact, but not solely by lack of attention. Their falsity has roots more substantial. As a matter of fact, it is akin to the birth of myths. In myths man seeks refuge. He does not mind by what device he contrives to meddle in them, whether by drugs, liquor or mere lying.\* Incapable of deep penetration of himself, he assumes a mask. Lying and forging like this provides momentary consolation, offering the minor distraction of a sort of charade. Man gets away for a while from what he experiences and what he sees. He invents. He transmogrifies. He mythifies. He creates. He pats himself on the back for being an artist. On a small scale he mimics the painters whom he charges with madness.

\*     \*     \*

Journalists know this, or sense it. The falsities of the press, the headlines by which they underline them, all flatter this thirst for unreality. Alas, there is no force in this world capable of supervising the metamorphosis of the work of reality into a work of art, but this dull transforming does at least provide the need for fables. Exactitude exasperates the mass of mankind, anxious to be fantastical. Has not our age invented the term *escapism*? Nevertheless, the only way really to escape from oneself is by allowing oneself to be occupied by some other force.

This is why fantasy is detestable. People confuse it with

---

\* *Falsehood is the only art form approved of by the general public, which instinctively prefers it to reality.*

Essay of Indirect Criticism.

poetry which is so shy that it tries to put garments over its algebraics. The realism of poetry is an impudent one. In the poet who discovers it, it is inherent, and he makes every effort never to betray it.

\*       \*       \*

Poetry is a religion without hope. In it the poet expends himself, knowing all the time that a masterpiece is after all but a number to a performing dog on a quicksand.

Admittedly, he finds consolation in the claim that his work plays its part in some more tangible mystery. But that hope comes from the fact that any man is a tenebrosity (bears tenebrosity within himself) and that the task of the artist must be to bring that tenebrosity into broad daylight. Further, this worldly night of his does furnish man in all his limitation with an extension having no precise limits, which is a solace to him. He comes to resemble a paralytic, sunk in slumber, dreaming he walks.

\*       \*       \*

Poetry is an ethic. By this I mean that it is a secret attitude, a discipline built up and maintained according to the aptitudes of a man who rejects the categorical imperative, which is an imperative putting all systems out of gear.

This private ethic can seem sheer immorality to those who deceive themselves or who live loosely so that to them falsity is truth and our truth their falsity.

It is in virtue of this principle that I once wrote that Genet is a moralist and "*I am a lie which always tells the truth*" is sweet grazing for asses. They roll in it. The phrase meant that socially man is a lie. It is particularly when he lines up against the simple truths of this and charges them with falsity that your poet tries to combat the social life.

No defence more savage than this of the plural against the singular. From their cages all the parrots repeat: "He is false. He is cheating us," just when one is making one's most

Such an ethic, taking form, therefore affronts. It will convince but those able to make themselves small before the great and those whose love is greater than their respect. It will rally neither electors nor admirers. It will make but friends.

*     *     *

If a savage feels fear, he sculps a god of fear and begs that god to take away his fear. He fears the god born of his fear. He exorcises his fear in the form of an object which becomes a work of art by the intensity of the fear and a deity because this object born of his weakness of ethic changes into a force commanding him to reform. This is precisely why a work of art born of a special ethic becomes a thing apart from the ethic, drawing from this solely an intensity likely often enough to produce the opposite conviction, even to the point of modifying the feelings in the artist in which it originated.

Certain philosophers discuss whether the gods are merely labelled by man or inspire him to give them name, that is, whether the poet invents or whether he obeys orders superior to his cult.

There is that old catchword about inspiration being merely perspiration. It is true that any poet is the recipient of orders. But these come from a tenebrosity which the centuries have piled up in him, and of which he is but the humble vehicle, tenebrosity into which, desiring progression into light, he cannot go.

It is this vehicle that he has to cherish, cleaning it, oiling it, keeping his eye on it, for ever checking up, so that it may ever be fit for the strange service he requires of it. It is the checking over of this vehicle (which should never be relaxed) that I call one's private ethic and to the requirements of which it is meet to submit, particularly when everything seems to show that this unrewarding obedience brings nothing but reproof.

To renounce the humility which such obedience implies is to have the pretension of excogitating things in one's own top-knot, substituting the ornamental for the implacable, classing oneself as superior to one's tenebrosities and, by the excuse of being pleasing, obeying others instead of forcing on them, to compel their belief, those gods which dwell within us.

It happens that this humility draws down on us the hatred of the incredulous, bringing against us charges of pride, of artifice and of heresy, even bringing us to the fires of public execution.

That is of little consequence. We should never for an instant withdraw from a task the more exacting to us since to justify it in our eyes it has only its inevitability, its permanent incomprehensibility and its refusal of hope.

Only the breed who crave cheap fame will place their hope in posthumous justice, no solace to a poet, who is not very credulous regarding earthly eternity, merely concerned to maintain his balance on the tight-rope from which it is his compatriots' main preoccupation to make him slip.

It must be this taut wire stretched above the great vacancy which results in our being regularly treated as mountebanks, and the emergence of our secrets into the light, a true labour of archaeological excavation, in our being mistaken for conjurors.

*       *       *

I have abandoned Paris. Paris cultivates the torture technique of Mexico, smearing its victims with honey, after which the ants have a field-day.

However, it so happens that ants do also eat each other, and that makes the use of veils a practicality.

I have left behind me the grey snow roads and here I am in the garden of this villa—Santo Sospiro—Sacred Sigh—is its name—I have tattooed them like living flesh. It is a real haven here, so efficiently has the young woman who owns it contrived her barriers of solitude.

The air seems wonderful, and on the greensward there are

windfalls of lemons. But alas, Paris sticks to one's soul, a black train still trails behind me. Patience will be necessary, to contain myself till that glue dries and its dead crusts of themselves flake away. So far, the iodine and the brine are taking over. The last stage will be when that mud of lies with which I am spattered from head to foot peels away from me.

The régime begins. Gradually it will turn into an Orestean purge. The epidermis of my soul again becomes clean.

\*       \*       \*

I am unquestionably the most obscure and the most celebrated of poets. Sometimes this makes me sad, for fame terrifies me and I like to excite only affection. My sadness must come from the mire with which we are all impregnated and against which I rebel. But as soon as I think upon it I scorn my melancholy, telling myself that my visibility, a product of idiotic legends, does protect my invisibility, wrapping it round with a thick, glittering coat of armour which can withstand any blows with impunity.

When they think to wound me they wound a stranger whom I prefer not to know and when they stick pins into a wax figurine of Jean Cocteau, that figure is so little like me that the postman delivers the witchcraft at the wrong address and it never touches me. Not that I boast in the least of being untouchable, merely that by quirk of fortune I can so arrange it that the vehicle which I happen to be is out of their reach.

\*       \*       \*

Formerly the artist was surrounded by a conspiracy of silence. The modern artist is surrounded by a conspiracy of hubbub. There is nothing that is not discussed and voided of value. France is beset by a drunken orgy of self-denigration. Like Nero, she takes her own life, crying: *What an artist I am assassinating!* She makes self-destruction a point of honour, trampling her own pride underfoot—a matter of pride. Her youth huddles in its basements, offering legitimate resistance to the scorn with which it is always met, except when it is made cannon fodder.

In the throes of such babelisation the poet should find happiness in composing and observing his own ethic, cut off as an innocent man who remains deaf to the charges levelled against him, makes no effort to prove his innocence, finds the crimes imputed delectable, and accepts his sentence of death. For this guiltless one takes due note that innocence becomes guilty by default and better be charged with a real crime regarding which he is defended than be wrongly accused of imaginary crimes against unreality where reality has no right of appeal.

\*     \*     \*

Art makes hallow the murder of the habitual. There is the neck the artist undertakes to wring.

Look at how our troubled age has got caught in the trap of painters, gradually making it the custom to compare any picture with other pictures, instead of comparing it with its subject. The result is that the intensity of the operation by which any subject is transformed into a work of art remains a dead letter to it. It is only moved by the shock of yet another resemblance, that which (in its view) non-representational pictures share by the mere fact that they avoid the old sort of resemblance, and these pictures it finds reassuring by a non-representational character *which it can recognise* and which it thinks is a triumph over representation. Whereas whether he chooses to make a magnificent disfigurement of the human features or to depict them just as they are, Picasso imparts to us a like intensity. He however is forgiven this because of the range of his voice and because people are ready to accept a breather on their Gadarene path. But Picasso is the only one allowed this. Which leads to hearing babble like that of a certain young man who at Vallauris had just seen his latest canvases and over the telephone said to me: "Astonishing canvases, even though representational."

That sort of young man is impervious to the painter who

tomorrow counters a cyclone by a calm, revives the representational by an intensity unobtrusive but subversive, all by a rebellion against the habitual of such power that no other painter dares risk being the victim of the event. If any does try to do so, without fail he will be muddle-headedly accounted a laggard, whereas what he will have done is but proof of superior courage.

The ethic of this victim-to-be must therefore be very compact, since his creation will gain no advantage from the conventional brand of being scandalous, his shocking behaviour being precisely that of not being shocking.

Ever since I surmounted the obstacle which concealed my road ahead from me, I have myself known this isolation. (I was then already well launched along wrong roads). What is more, to all my fellow-writers about me my leap across was a fall and their first reaction was that it was like climbing in over the wall of a private park full of dangerous dogs.*

* *Having been an habitué at Marcel Proust's, at an age no greater than his when he was writing* Les Plaisirs et les Jours, *I saw him—which I found normal—treat me as if I had got over that stage and was already on the hard road which one day I was to take and which he himself had already taken. Doubtless Proust, able like none other to perceive the structure of a life, saw farther than I did down that future which kept everything from me, the more so since I thought my immediate present primary, whereas later I was to look upon it as a succession of grievous errors. The explanation of his indulgence towards me is to be found on p.* 122 *of* A l'ombre des Jeunes Filles en fleur.

*This is the reason why so many of Proust's letters seemed incomprehensible to me, dipping as they did into a future clear to him but out of my reach.*

*His room was a dark-room in which he developed his negatives in a human time system in which future and past inter-mingled. I profit by that, and I have at times regretted having known Marcel at a period in which, however much I respected his work, I was still unfit to enjoy it.*

*That solitude lasts, and I fit in with it. Every time, the work in hand comes up against what matters, is born suspect. I was trained in this school by Raymond Radiguet, then fifteen. He used to say: "We must write novels like everybody else. We must contradict the vanguard. That is now the only cursed position. The only one worth anything."*

The varied nature of what I produced saved me from turning myself into a habit. That varied nature, however, thoroughly put off superficial minds following those extremes of fashion which boast they are not fashionable. It gave the impression that I took advantage of the fashions without understanding them, just when I was in fact contradicting them in books, plays, and films, up against a select band both blind and deaf. For even though they divest themselves of their individuality, the common run of people never really reject individualism and in a hall can easily be taken by an idea which in a room would set their backs up. Not being the prey of snob notions, ordinary folk almost always knew by their noses what I was after. In the field of stage or screen that of course goes without saying. An audience which has paid its entrance money is not prejudiced, compacted together its members electrify each other, are all reception, not cutting themselves off from the spectacle as does the specially invited man, for he comes wearing a mack guaranteed to keep out any grace.

Thus I counted as a trifler, dispersing myself too widely, whereas really from various angles I was all the time poking my same little light into the odd corners of the solitude of the human being—and of free will.

*       *       *

Free will is the result of the infinite co-existence of opposites conjugally united, interplaited, fused in one. Man feels free to choose because he hesitates between alternatives which are parts of the same unity, but which he separates out to his own ends. Left or right? It's all one. For all the sly appearance of opposition, either track is related to the other. That is why man is all self-questioning, asking himself if he is right or wrong, whereas he is neither one nor the other and without being free merely seems to choose one or other juxtaposed general course out of the complex tissue which however stable looks as if fortuitous.

*       *       *

I have remarked that my invisibility was in danger of becoming visible when at some distance. This is in countries where I am judged through the medium of translations even when these are poor, instead of having my work judged, as it is in my own country, through the prism of a personality invented for me.

But that all remains imprecise. To be quite frank, it rather seems to me that the visible plays some part in the interest taken in me from afar off, and that it is my false personality that rouses interest. I find this so whenever I travel and people are disconcerted, meeting me in the flesh, so different is the man that confronts them from the poster Cocteau.

When all's said and done, the best thing for me is to let the whole confusion be. For it is not so easy to get the personality-vehicle or the vehicle of one's work started, and works of art imitate the frenzied liberty of all offspring, their one thought to race about in promiscuous prostitution.

*            *            *

Inwardly and outwardly, the birth of works of art is menaced by a thousand dangers. What is the individual? A starry tenebrosity of cells in suspense in a magnetic fluidity, subject to gravity just like those living or dead cells which we call stars, the intermediate spaces of which have their replica in ourselves.

Apparently, cancer comes from a disorder of our magnetic medium (our heavens) and a grain of intrusive sand in the astral mechanism which that fluid supports.

A magnet groups iron filings in faultless pattern, like those of frost, like insect designs, like flowers. Introduce a foreign body (a hair-pin, for instance), between one of the terminals of the magnet and the filings, and the pattern forms so as to leave one vacant place, *which is not that where the pin is*, but is such as to produce a local anarchy of the filings, piling them up shapelessly at a dead point.

Where are we to find the pin to be introduced into ourselves.

Alas, our internal patterning is too fluid, too unaccountable, too subtle. If a man's thumb were not all inter-stellar space, it would weigh many thousand tons. That makes the enquiry a delicate one. Seeing that the universal machinery is the same, must be of high simplicity, its matter a kaleidoscopic triad*. The phenomenon is thus the same in our realms, where the least straw introduced may cause an anarchy of thought, a disorganisation of the atomic structure of the gravitational systems essential to a work of art.

The most minute foreign body on a terminal of our magnet, and our work becomes cancerous.

Fortunately, the moment our spirit loses its way, our organism's bristles are up, thereby avoiding for us that disease which might eat up a work and destroy the very stuff of it. I have told in *Opium* how my novel *les Enfants Terribles* let me down because I got involved in "purposive writing."

Often enough a pin the origin of which is unknown to us, by an anarchy which is almost one of our very cells, causes in a work a real disease of circumstance, so that books come to reveal what their author really wanted of them.

Apart from the unpredictable obstacles of our very fluid, the least interposition of the volitional threatens to harm the occult powers in us which require to assume a passive role, yet at the same time be active and attentive, providing them with a framework fitting in with human dimensions. One can guess what supervision we should maintain in that half-sleep which lies between consciousness and the unconscious, a supervision always threatening to be too vigilant, which, robbing a work of its transcendental quality, or being too feeble, can leave it in a dream condition, cut off from other men.

\*          \*          \*

* *Possibly, by the invention of the kaleidoscope, we put our finger on a great secret. For its infinite combinations derive from there elements which at first sight seem to be alien one to the others : a rotation, some fragments of glass, and a mirror, the last of these lending the other two organisation.*

Man is a sick creature. I mean that he is constrained by his limiting dimensions, which prevent his comprehension either of the infinite or of non-existent dimensions.

More than by any science it is by the shame which this infirmity inflicts him with and by the obsession of escape therefrom that he comes to conceive the inconceivable, or at least, to admit that the machinery in which he occupies a humble place was not designed for his use.*

Man even comes to recognise that eternity can neither have been, nor be becoming, that it is in some way fixed, ever being, in fact, and content to be, that minutes are equal to centuries and centuries to minutes and there are really neither, nothing but a terrifying, swarming, vibrant motionlessness against which his pride strains ultimately to the point of coming to the belief that his own paltry globe is the only world and he the lord of it.

He tones down, but the suspicion that the trifle which he inhabits is merely a grain of dust in the milky way he nevertheless rejects. He spurns the painful certainty that our cells within us are as distant each from each and as ignorant of us as are the stars. He finds it disagreeable to remind himself that he may be dwelling on the still warm crust of a cinder fallen from the sun, that this cinder is rapidly cooling and that it is a kind of illusory perspective which drags the speed out to the extent of a few thousand million centuries. (I shall come back to perspectives of this sort later).

It is fighting off a pessimism understandable enough that has made man invent certain games, to take his mind off things on the journey from birth to death.

Even if he is a believer (little worthy, for that matter, of

---

* According to Calligaris, epidermal stimuli at certain points (for instance, the touch of a cold point on the posterior surface of the right leg, about $2\frac{1}{2}$ cms. in from the axial line and about 3–4 cms. above the mid-point of the leg) releases reflexes which tend to deceive us as to the time-space complex, giving the illusion that one has become a visionary. Subsequently, one finds that the things one speaks of do come about.

either rewards or punishments out of all proportion to his merits) his principal remedy against pessimism is to believe that his journey's end has in store for him either a glorious triumph or tortures which he still finds preferable to the idea of being no longer anything at all.

To conquer his discomfort at belonging to the incomprehensible, he tries to make it comprehensible. Thus, for example, the massacre and slaughter for which he wishes to assume responsibility he puts down to patriotism, whereas all they are is the annoying tendency of our globe to stir up its fleas from time to time and lick its sores.

This is so true that science, which with its right hand looks after pests, with its left hand invents destructive weapons, prompted thereto by nature, which does not seek the salvation of its victims but assistance in making more, till it balances its herds of human stock just as it balances the volumes of its waters.

It just so happens that the brief periods between one and another of the spasms by which the contorted face of the earth shakes up its lay-out of land, changing outlines, sea depths and mountain heights, seem long.

*          *          *

Nature is naive. Maurice Maeterlinck has told the story of the very tall plant which made its seed parachutes and still goes on turning them out, despite the fact that degeneration has long since made a dwarf thing of it. At Cap Nègre I have seen wild oranges which had been domesticated turn wild again and thrust up long thorns in the small area menaced by the shadow of a palm-tree. The least sunshine is enough to cheat the sap which stupidly exposes itself to the least frost. And so on.

The mistake must be in trying to understand what is happening on all floors of the edifice.

It is to this pre-adamic curiosity that we owe progress, which is no more than stubbornness about the error of choice,

and a tendency to extend that error to its ultimate con-
sequences.

\*      \*      \*

On a globe madly set on self-destruction it is surprising that
art should survive and that manifestations of it which should
be considered luxury things (and which certain mystics for
this very reason would abolish) maintain their prerogatives,
interesting so many people and turning into a stock exchange.
Money circles having observed that thought is saleable,
gangs are formed to cash in on the phenomenon. One lot
think out the works of art, the others exploit them. The result
is that money becomes more abstract than intelligence. It is
not often that intelligence gets anything out of it.

Epoch in which bankrupts monkey with low-level
invisibility known as fraud.

"The treasury robs me, I shall rob the treasury," that is
how the business go-between reasons. His imagination is more
lively than that of the artist whom he exploits. He becomes
*sui generis* a great artist. He saves that balance which is only
preserved by imbalance and traffic. If he did not cheat, the
blood of a nation addicted to hoarding would coagulate and
cease circulation.

\*      \*      \*

Nature issues orders, men disobey them. She manages to
get them in step by using their trickery to de-equalise levels
which tend to even out. She is as crafty as a wild creature.
With apparently an equal passion for life and murder, she
thinks but of her belly and the pursuit of an invisible task, the
visible aspect of which reveals her absolute indifference
regarding what the individual goes through. Individuals do
not see things in the same way. They would like to be
responsible and sensitive. For instance, when an old woman
is trapped under ruins, when a submarine goes down, when
a speleologist falls into a crevasse, when an aircraft is lost in

the snow. When, in fact, disaster has human features. *When it is after men's own image.* But when disaster piles noughts on the figure, when it becomes anonymous, when it is disindividualised, individuals lose all interest in it unless they happen to be afraid lest it may flood over the edges of the anonymous zone to which they have relegated it, and menace them personally.

It is much the same with the airman who bombs a world so far reduced in scale that an effort of the imagination is required to bring it into relation with ordinary human scales. The inhumanity of the men who drop the bombs comes from their failure to conceive of the scale, hence thinking they are bombing a sort of toy world in which no real individual could live or move about.

It does of course happen that the human imagination of an airman comes into action just when he is about to destroy inhumanly. The book by the pilots who dropped the bombs on Hiroshima and Nagasaki offers us an example of this.* But they too were acting under orders and those orders derived from yet other orders which arose in the invisible and served the machinery which concerns me here, that which shuffles the cards of responsibility.

But apart from pride it is responsibility that compels man to account himself responsible and, seeking excuses, to go on serving invisibility. For, if he offers to suppress atomic weapons, that is not to make war impossible, but to make it possible. Self-devouring nature whispers this advice to him till it succeeds in convincing him that the atomic weapon would curtail his misfortunes.

\*          \*          \*

My argument is that we imagine danger (to ourselves) in a flimsy marriage between secret orders and the artificial

---

* *The bomb-droppers were M. Miller and A. Spitzer. Their machine was called* The Great Artist.

orders superimposed on them. Nature herself (obtuse in all conscience) is completely lost in it, losing her way in zig-zags which lead to crashes, after which, picking herself up from amid the confusion of our corpses, she continues her mad "bull" rush forward.

These catastrophes are food for astrologers, who write them down against the stars, whereas really they happen because of the starriness of ourselves, really being nebulae. Their reckonings would be just as valid if they swapped their telescopes for microscopes and pointed the instruments at themselves, when indeed they might hit upon the astrological marks of our enslavement.

Relative enslavement, as a matter of fact, to which we must return later.

We pay a great deal of attention to ourselves. To take advantage of this discharge is too simple and it is too easy to make out to oneself that one is not responsible for acts which upset those expected of us (and offend our obscurity).

In that symphony of opprobrium which rends my ears, which faults were my own? Did I not lay myself open?

The time has come to descend from the heights. Since I am addressing friends who read me, perhaps I owe it to them to look myself in the face and instead of being accuser, become accused. Perhaps it is right for me to charge myself.

Of what? Of countless errors which are not content with bringing outward and visible thunderbolts down on me, but also inner ones. Countless little errors, disastrous faults once one has resolved not to commit them, but to respect one's own ethic.

Often have I slithered down the slope of things visible and seized the staff it offered me. I should have been hard. I was feeble. I thought myself out of reach. I thought: my armour protects me all right, I'm not going to mend the gaps in it. They turned into gaping breaches, open to the enemy.

Instead of grasping that the public consists of livestock able to clap with its front hooves, I allowed applause to seduce me. I kept telling myself that they offset the hostile cliques. I committed the crime of getting hot under the collar about insults and considering praise as my due.

Enjoying good health, I found this all natural and did not spare my strength. Falling ill, I found it unbearable and rebelled against my lot.

All that little fits an inflexible ethic. The disgust I felt when I realised this cast me into a pessimism with the sight of which I regaled my friends. I tended to demoralise them. I stubbornly tried to persuade them how impotent they were to cure me. A scurrilous activity in which I engaged with fury till the rage of the invisible was set loose, to shame me. And that all happened from one minute to another, so that my friends came to wonder whether I was not tormenting them all for nothing.

Bathed in the sunshine of the coast where I live, I cast shadow about me. Spilling some ink about brings me back my calm, except when I try to decide whether the ink emerges from my pen or my veins. Then pessimism wins ahead, and optimism falls back. The return of pessimism I attribute to the liberties which I try to take with my work. I make those round me unhappy. When I reproach myself for it, I go tense instead of relaxing, which would be the least act of consideration for others.

The mail arrives. A packet from town. A hundred envelopes fall out, stamped with the stamps of the world. My pessimism becomes unlimited. What? I shall have to read and answer all those letters? I have never had a secretary. I write my letters myself and open my own hall door. People drop in. Am I not motivated by a fateful desire to please? Is it not fear lest people should begin to shun me? And there I begin to wrestle with the fear of losing my time and with remorse about the unwritten letters which thereby suffer.

If I reply, there will be a reply to my reply. If I stop replying, there will be reproaches. If I avoid any reply, there is regret. I am sure that my heart will win the day. But I am wrong. For it is weakness that wins against the true duties of my heart. Do I not owe my neighbour something? I am robbing him of these moments. What is more, I am also stealing time from those forces whose servant I am. They take their revenge for any addition I make to tasks marginal to my proper work.

A fine kettle of fish. And I charge myself with meddling in things with would-be occult energy, making unwise pronouncements, getting intoxicated with monologues, abandoning myself to endless rigmaroles in which I get lost.

And I then take up my own defence: Is not this verbal debauchery the only way in which, having no real brain, I can excite myself to the dizziness of composition? If I do not stimulate the machinery, I find it turns vegetal, thinks of nothing. That vacancy appals me and I lose myself in rhetoric.

After that, I go to bed. Instead of escapism by the printed word, I seek the escapism of sleep, sleep with dreams, mine being of extreme complexity and such real irreality that I sometimes confuse them with what is real.

All this contributes to making the borderline between responsibility and irresponsibility, visibility and invisibility, very uncertain.

I come to ask whether I am not just stupid, whether the intellect ascribed to me (and with which I am reproached) is not merely a mirage of unknown origin.

What with all the flashes of intuition, the acts of obedience and of disobedience, the crises of courage and of weariness, the clumsiness and the agilities—to the point of acrobatic recoveries just as I am tumbling down all my stairs—I am, you see, rather stupid, inscrutable to others and to myself, just like one of those princes with an ability to go on parade asleep, eyes wide open.

Have I perhaps been confusing rectitude with that passive obedience which couples one's wheel to the wheel of one's weaknesses? Have I perhaps imposed on my ethic a dead

C

road, a blind alley into which my intellect refuses to follow me? Have I not steered my skiff badly under the pretext of its being essential to be a bad helmsman? Have I not been shipwrecked on a desert island? Do others refuse to see me, or is it merely my signals that they do not see?

*          *          *

I am not in the childhood stage, but nearly so. My childhood lasts for ever. That is what gives the illusion that I have stayed young, whereas youth and infancy are not to be confused. Picasso says: *It takes a very long time to become young.* Youthfulness expels our childhood. In the long run, childhood reassumes its rights.

My mother died a child. She did not become infantile. She was a very active elderly child. She recognised me, but *her* childhood put me in place in *mine*, without, which was quite proper, our two childhoods merging one into the other. A little girl advanced in years, seated with all her childlike acts all round her, asked a little boy advanced in years about his school and counselled him to be good there tomorrow.

It is feasible that I too have this lengthy childhood, disguised as adulthood, from my mother, whom I resemble, possible too that this is the cause of all my misfortunes. Possible moreover that the invisible makes use of this. Certainly to the fact I owe certain verbal finds which are those of children, in whom there is no sense of the ridiculous. The words of children which get quoted are close to the dissociated words of poets, and there are some of them which I should be proud to have uttered.

But what nobody will admit in us is a mixture of childhood and age, unless it be as a way of being spoiled. But I am not at all like that. Sometimes I am scolded and upbraided without people realising that they are talking to me in the way families talk to children.

I am, in a phrase, a damned nuisance. There is no doubt about it, this is enough evidence to charge my cabbage with poisoning my goat, after first charging my goat with eating my cabbage.

Such is man. In him you have a vehicle not easy to use. It is normal for man the vehicle to exasperate the tenebrosity which is striving to acquire form. Certainly I, in my stupidity hinder it.

Even here, under this Nice sunshine, I find myself again becoming the pessimist or the optimist I always was, according to whether I lean to right or left.

I come to wonder whether it would be feasible for things to be otherwise and if my difficulty of being, if these errors which hamper my progression, are not really that progression itself and a regret at having not having had a different one. A fortune to which I have to submit just as I do to my body. Whence these bouts of pessimism and optimism, the permutations of which bespatter me. Systole and diastole of the universal beat of things.

That too makes us inclined to be melancholy about people dying and delighted by births, whereas our real condition is one of absolute non-being.

From this vacancy, this non-existence evolves our pessimism. Our optimism comes from a sensibility which counsels us to make the best of the parenthesis offered by this vacancy, taking advantage of it without seeking the key to a rebus in which man will never have the last word, for the good reason that there is no last word, our celestial system is no more lasting than our internal universe, duration is but a pretty story, vacancy is not vacancy, eternity tricks us, offering us the passage of time, whereas the compact which is at once space and time is a motionlessness in explosion, remote from any notion of either space or time.

*       *       *

In short, man is most braggart, and none should dare suggest that our system may hold either in the point of a pin or in the organism of any individual. Renan alone dared to say it, with a rather terrible little sentence: It is quite possible that the truth is sad.]

\*       \*       \*

Art should take crime as model. The prestige enjoyed by the criminal would be quite unimpressive were he not visible, did he not bring his jobs off. His fame is subject to the condition of losing, unless he should burgle or kill for the glory of losing and crime were nothing to him without the apotheosis of punishment.

\*       \*       \*

[The puzzle of the visible and invisible retains its puzzling elegance. It is impossible to solve it in a world fascinated by present happenings and devoid of anything to fall back on.] It does not favour trade. It obeys a rhythm which contradicts the rhythm of society, for that rhythm is very advanced in years and uses rouge. Never was speed slower. Madame de Staël moved from one end of Europe to the other faster than we do and Caesar conquered the Gauls in a week.

\*       \*       \*

[ I find it difficult to write this chapter. Since our French tongue is made from a number of differing languages, it happens that we are as badly understood in France as if we wrote a foreign language. I know men who hate reading Montaigne and get lost in him, whereas to me he speaks a tongue in which the smallest word has meaning. On the other hand, I sometimes have to go back to it twice before I can understand the sense of a newspaper article. I have few words at my service. I piece them together till I get a sort of meaning out of them. But the force which drives me to write is an impatient one. It hustles me on. That does not make things any easier. In addition, I avoid the terminology used by learned men and philosophers, a terminology which is still a foreign tongue, difficult to follow for those whom I address. True, those whom I address also have their own tongue, which is not mine. The invisible has something to do with that, also pessimism. For it can happen that one gets an urge to join in happy rounds and the dancers do not turn away from one.]

\*　　　\*　　　\*

If this book falls into the hands of some attentive young man, my advice to him is to put on the brake, re-reading any sentence read too quickly, giving a bit of thought to all the trouble I am giving myself to capture waves which scorn the chaos of the milieux which make him suffer and which he tries to escape. I beg him to try to escape from that plural which rejects him to the singular which offers its own darkness. I do not say, like Gide: "Set out, abandoning family and home." My words to him are: "Stay at home, [but escape into tenebrosity. Inspect that, then in broad daylight reveal what you find."]

[I do not ask him to be interested in my waves, but by contact with the vehicle from which they issue, to learn to make himself one which fits him and is capable of uttering his particular waves. For what the fire of youth lacks is the ground frame which such a vehicle gives. This I find in countless fragments of writing which comes to my hands.]

\*　　　\*　　　\*

One should not confuse the tenebrosity of which I speak and that into which Freud asked his patients to descend. Freud burgled poverty-stricken dwellings. Out of them he got a few pieces of wretched furniture and a few erotic pictures. He never sanctified the transcendental in the abnormal. He did not offer a welcome to the great disorders. He offered the pestiferous, a private confessional.

A lady of New York confided to me her friendship for Marlene Dietrich. When I praised Marlene's heart of gold, this dame said: "*That isn't it. She listens to me.*" Yes, in a city which likes neither to complain nor to be complained to and by an instinctive defence gesture bungs up its ears against the catching disease of confidences, Marlene, who is such a patient soul, listened to this woman. The good lady got it out of her system on the cheap. Elsewhere, preying on the tiresome, the psychiatrists take the job on. I am all for their charging high fees.

The Freudian key to dreams is most naive. Simple things are dubbed complex. Freud's obsession with sex was bound to seduce an idle society to which sex is the king-pin of life. American investigations show that the plural remains the plural when it turns singular to declare what vices it has invented. In the confession of vices and the parading of virtues there is identical idiocy.

It is easy to get at Freud. His hell (his purgatory) is scaled down to fit the mass of mankind. In distinction from this study of ours, all Freud wants is visibility.

The tenebrosity which engages me is different. It is a treasure cave. By courage—and the right password—it may be opened, not by either a doctor or a neurotic. But if the treasures make us forget the *Open Sesame*, it is a dangerous cave.

It is from this cave, from this luxury wreck, this *drawing-room at the bottom of a lake*, that all great souls draw their riches.

As you may have guessed, sexuality does of course play some part there too. Vinci and Michael-Angelo prove that. But their secrets have nothing to do with the house-movings of Sigmund Freud.*

The vulture mimicked in the folds of the Virgin's gown in

---

* *The trial of the old enchanter, as Nietzsche used to say, a trial in which Emile Ludwig plays the part of state prosecutor, incriminates neither the discoveries of Dr. Breuer, nor the progress of the psycho-analysts and psychiatrists. They no longer seek their own illnesses in sick people. They look after them.*

Leonardo da Vinci's picture, like the glandular *sac* under the arm of the young man in the Sixtine Chapel, are examples of the double concealments in which geniuses have taken delight. During the Renaissance, their origin was not in complexes, but in the malicious intent of tricking the dictatorial police of the Church. In a way these are quite important pieces of dupery. They are more denunciatory of the childishness which the painters maintained than are any fixed notions. They are addressed more to friends than to the analyst, and of no greater Freudian consequence than the pupils' signatures which the microscope has discovered in the nostrils and ears of Rubens' women.

As for the Oedipus Complex, Freud would be in almost perfect agreement with our line (human tenebrosity hustling us into one trap under pretext of avoiding another), had Sophocles not believed in exterior fate. The Gods find it great fun to cook up a frightful practical joke, of which Oedipus is the victim.

This frightful comedy I complicated in *la Machine Infernale*, turning Oedipus's victory over the Sphinx into a false triumph born of his pride and of the weakness of personality of the Sphinx, a half-divine, half-feminine creature, who, to enable him to avoid death, offers him the solution of the conundrum. The Sphinx acts here as the princess was to act in my film *Orpheus*, when she thinks herself condemned for the crime of free-will. The Sphinx, intermediary between the Gods and men, is duped by the Gods, who pretend to leave it free and suggest to it saving Oedipus just to ruin him.

Precisely by this betrayal of the Sphinx I underline to what extent the drama is in the Greek conception outside Oedipus, and in *Orpheus* I develop this idea further. The Gods prompt the death of Orpheus to ruin him, making him immortal and blind, *so robbing him of his muse.*

Freud's error is to have turned our tenebrosity into a protection for bits of furniture, and this discredits it. His mistake is to have thrown it open whereas, being bottomless, it can never be fully open to us.

* * *

I have frequently been reproached with giving up so little in my works to Nature. This is, first, because phenomena interest me far more than their results, it is the supernatural in the natural which primarily impresses me. Further, how many, many others have done it better than I could, and what overweening pride it would have been to imagine one could beat Colette at it. On wing or petal, in wasp or tiger, it is the secret of the markings which prompts my pen. The other invisible side intrigues me more than the visible. This leaning of mine impels me to lively enjoyment of things without any attempt to communicate my delight.

( Each of us owes it to himself to remain within his own prerogatives and not to tread in the fields of others ) Mine are to be seen consisting in a tendency not to be satisfied till on my desk a void begins to look as if it were full.

That is the complete explanation of this ledger, in which neither the picturesque, nor science, nor philosophy, nor psychology can find their column.

Thus, between two chairs, I try to re-bottom a third, that phantom chair of which I speak in my foreword.

* * *

P.S. ( The taste for responsibility. Most lively in certain childhoods subject to family scorn. Such childhood confesses to acts of which it is utterly incapable (which remains to be proved, since such responsibility may be unconscious).

It is not rare for children to take on themselves phenomena which trouble haunted houses  Nor is it rare for such phenomena to result from their intention to surprise, which may be the explanation of childishness  A force emanates from them, acting and then seeming to compromise them, by driving them to confess to parents or police what they never realise has all come out of their own head. In both the visible and the invisible they would like to play a part.

But the tenebrosity of such children is still somnolent. Ours is wide awake. It is capable of conceiving real tumours, monstrous pregnancies. And, as the following chapter will show, it is capable of impregnating us with creatures deriving from exorcism.

# On the Birth of a Poem

I HAVE just been the ground of one of those Ravaillac
experiments, all open to a conflict of forces which in poets
are so many Places de Grèves, teams of horses pulling at
me two ways. Having resolved to turn to examing the birth
of one of my poems—*L'Ange Heurtebise*—The Angel Heurtebise—apt, so I imagined, to illustrate the relationships of the
consci͏ ͏ and unconscious, the visible and the invisible, I
suddenly found I could not write at all. Words dried up,
words jostled, words intertangled, piled up, took possession of
each other, like so many diseased cells. As they came from
my pen they assumed attitudes which made it impossible for
then to fit in with each other and make a sentence. I became
stubborn, ascribed it all to that artificial seeing-through-
things which I endeavoured to set up in opposition to my
tenebrosity. I reached the point of thinking I should never
get free from it all, or that advancing years were rusting up
my vehicle which would be worse, for, free or not, I saw
myself unable to claim I could do any other sort of work. I
rubbed out, I tore up, I started over again. Every time, the
same dead end, every time up against the same obstruction.
I was about to give up, when lying on the table I came
upon my book *Opium*. I opened it by chance (if I dare use the
word) and read a paragraph which enlightened me regarding
my incapability. My memory was getting things wrong,
confusing dates, forcing gears, ruining the mechanism. And,
without my noticing it, a more profound memory had risen
up against me and taken a stand against my errors.

False perspective had placed me as if in a certain situation prior to another, whereas it was after. Thus are our past acts foreshortened as we withdraw from them and their orchestration falls victim to a false note, to false witness given by the man pleading his own cause.

*          *          *

Before *L'Ange Heurtebise*, in my writings the symbol angel had ceased to bear any specific relationship to certain religious imagery, notwithstanding that long ago el Greco the Greek deidiotised the term, according it new meaning and in Spain drew on himself the thunderbolts of the Inquisition.

There should be an approximation to the concept in what the crew of Superfortress No. 42,7353 saw after they had dropped the first atomic bomb. They speak of purple light and a pillar of indescribable shades of colour, but add that then words failed them. The sight they saw is for ever locked within them.

*          *          *

There is a similarity between the words angel and angle—in French angel—*ange*—becomes *angle* if one adds an "l" (or wing, for *aile*, pronounced "el" in French, means wing). This is perhaps a trick of French (to some measure of English too), if one dare assert that in such things there is chance. Further, in Yiddish the word angel and angle become synonymous,* which makes the Biblical fall of the angels mean the collapse of the angles, that is, the very human creation of a conventional sphere. Voided of its geometrical soul, turned into an interlacing of hypotheuses and right-angles, the sphere rests exclusively on points which ensure its radiance.

Further, I knew that the important thing was to avoid the collapse within ourselves of that geometric soul. To lose either angels or angles is a danger to which persons with their feet too squarely on the ground are subject.*

* *The author in fact suggests that angels and angles are synonymous in Hebrew, a prophetic essay in implicit astrophysics or molecular structure— even water owing its fantastic properties to such peculiarities as the angles*

Genesis lacks any reference to the fall of the angels, but we may mention that those troublesome legendary creatures are said to have fecundated the daughters of man whereby they brought forth giants. This would mean that somewhere in Jewish imagination giants and angels became confused. Gustave Doré has wonderfully depicted that avalanche of bodies through wild gorges which they fill with their muscular but topsy-turvy frames.

Whence the visual notion of the angel? Was it the human shape assumed by those inhuman creatures? Or was it not almost certainly the longing in man to make certain forces understandable, to master an abstract presence, to incarnate this so as in it to find some semblance of himself and thereby suffer less fear of it?

The natural phenomena of thunder, eclipses, and floods would be less awesome if originating in a visible flock of beings instructed by the Almighty.

If like men, the individual beings of such a band would lose that vagueness which the mind dislikes, that nameless something which terrifies children in the dark and brings them rushing breathless to any light.

It was in this spirit, though minus the tenebrosities of the Book of Revelations, that the Greek gods were born. Each either made a vice real or magnified a virtue. They moved to and from between Mt. Olympus and Athens as if between one floor and another of an apartment building. They were most reassuring. Whereas angels must have been an embodiment of fear.

Graceful but cruel monsters, terribly male yet bi-sexed, such is the notion I used to get of flying angels—or angles—

---

*subtended by its hydrogen arms, which stand not at 90 degrees but at 104 degrees—too anachronistic to be true. And yet does not the word* tseir *signify both a heavenly messenger and the socket in which the pin of a bronze age door works—and did not modern Israel achieve a youth movement which thus called it itself "the angles of Zion"? Madame Chance is an artful lady—A.B.*

till I had proof that their invisibility could be embodied in a poem and made visual *without any risk of being visible.*

My play *Orpheus* was originally to have been a tale of Joseph and the Virgin, the tittle-tattle they suffered through the activities of the angel (a carpenter's assistant), the spite of Nazareth about an inexplicable pregnancy, and the way that spite forced the couple to flee the place.

This plot lent itself to so many misunderstandings that I gave it up. In its place I took the Orphic theme, in which the place of the birth of the divine infant is taken by the inexplicable birth of poetry.

Here too, an archangel was to have played a part, disguised as a glazier, but I was not to write the act till much later at Villefranche's *Hotel Welcome*. Then once again I was free to disguise the angel in blue dungarees, with glass wings on his back. Some years later, he ceased to be an angel at all and became an unimportant young man who was dead, the chauffeur of the princess in my film. (That is why the journalists get it all wrong and call the chauffeur an angel).

If I rather run ahead, that is solely to make it quite clear that the character of the angel enjoyed a platonic existence within me and caused me no trouble whatsoever till I came to that poem. Indeed, even when I had finished this, it (or he) was still inoffensive enough. I preserved his name solely in the play and the film. When it came to the poem it was of little import whether I dealt with him or not.

Now, here is the paragraph of *Opium* which opened my eyes to my impotence to write this chapter. The incident dates from 1928, but I had put down: 1930!

"One day when I was going to see Picasso in la Boétie Street, I had the notion in the lift that I was growing larger side by side with something quite terrible, which would also be eternal. A voice dinned in my ear: 'My name is on the board.' This shock brought me to my senses, and on the brass switch-board I read these words: *The Heurtebise Lift.*

"I recall that when I got to Picasso our talk was of miracles.

Picasso insisted that everything was miraculous. It was miraculous, he said, that one did not melt in one's bath."

From a distance I can see how those words influenced me. They epitomise the style of a play in which miracles were not to be miracles, in which indeed they were to be both comic and tragic, also if possible as intriguing as the world of grown-ups is for children.

I though no more of that lift incident. Suddenly the whole situation changed. My play lost its outlines. At night I went to sleep, only to waken with a start and be unable to get off again. By day I was all gloom, wading through a quagmire of dreams. These tribulations became frightful. The angel was within me without my realising it. And what was wanting *was that name Heurtebise*, which was gradually taking possession of me, insisting on my becoming aware of it.

By dint of hearing that name, hearing it without hearing it, hearing its pattern, if I can put it like that, and being in a sort of realm in which stopping one's ears was impossible, by dint thus of hearing the silence bawl that name at the top of its voice, by dint of being harried by the name, I remembered that cry in the lift: "My name is on the board" and I thereupon christened the angel who since he had already christened himself and I was not doing it at all, was indignant at my obtuseness.

Thus giving him a name, I thought he might leave me in peace. How wrong I was! The mythical creature now became unbearable. He was constantly under my feet, disporting himself crazily and banging at me, so to speak, like a child in the womb. I had to bear absolute torture, for that angel harried me incessantly, till I resorted to opiates, thinking to calm him by such devices. But he was not at all pleased at that, and made me pay a fine price.

Today, on such a genial shore, I find it difficult to reconstitute the details of that period or the degrading symptons. We have a gift of forgetting the bad, which is our safeguard. Nevertheless, our profound memories are always awake, and that is why we may remember a gesture of our childhood more clearly than anything we have just done. By stirring up such double memories, I can get myself into a state inconceivable to those who do not know the rites of a poet. Thus insidiously, having boasted of being free and absolutely disobedient to all that, once again I found myself under orders and my pen raced away. Nothing any longer cramped it. I dwell in Anjou Street. My mother is alive. I perceive my troubles on her features. She asks no questions. She suffers. So do I. And the angel mocks us. He prances about like a mad thing. "Have yourself exorcised," somebody says. "You are possessed by the devil." Not at all. By an angel. An entity seeking shape, one of those who, it seems, some other realm denies access to our own, but are drawn by curiosity, resorting to all manner of tricks, just to get a foothold.

\*          \*          \*

The angel was scarcely bothered at all by my obstreperousness. I was but its vehicle, and it treated me as such. It was preparing its sally. My crises grew more frequent, till they turned into one continuous crisis comparable to the early pangs of confinement. But a monstrous childbirth, never to benefit by the maternal instinct and the confidence which this engenders. Imagine a parthenogenesis, male and female, united in one body, giving birth. At last, after a night in which I contemplated suicide, in Anjou Street this child was ejected from the womb. Parturition had lasted seven days, during which the callous indifference of the creature exceeded all bounds, for it made me write against the grain.

\*          \*          \*

What emerged from me and was inscribed on the pages of a sort of album, bore no likeness to the Mallarméan jelly or the golden thunderbolt of a Rimbaud, neither to automatic writing or anything else I ever knew. The moves were made as in a game of chess, the structure suggesting alexandrines breaking and re-knitting together at their own whim. It set a temple cock-eyed, measuring up pillars, colonnades, cornices, volutes, architraves, making mistakes, starting all over again. It clouded frosted glass, it criss-crossed lines, right-angle triangles, hypothenuses, diameters. It added, it multiplied, it divided. It drew on my most intimate memories to humanise its equations. It seized merely the scruff of the neck, forced me down over the paper, and I had to obey the rhythm of my insufferable invader and bend myself to the service which he demanded of my ink, that flowing stream of ink down which as on a river he floated his way into poetry. I kept myself going with the hope that he would relieve me of his hampering personality and take another form, one exterior to my personality. A lot I cared about his aim. The essential was—passive obedience to his process of transformation. Assistance would be saying too much, for he seemed to despise me and not to expect any aid of me. There was no longer any question of sleep or personal existence. It was merely his deliverance and my own, of which, as far as that goes, he did not care a fig.

On the seventh day (it was seven in the evening), Heurtebise at last became a poem and liberated me. I was in a state of stupefaction. I examined the shape the angel had taken. I still found it distant, haughty, absolutely indifferent to whatever was not just it. A monstrosity of egotism. A block of invisibility.

That invisibility, compacted of angels which emit fire, that ship ice-bound, that iceberg with water all about it, will for ever remain invisible. Thus the angel Heurtebise decided. His earthly outlines lacking for him the sense they have for us. People do make theses on it, they do write about it, but despite all the exegesis, it all remains concealed. As the phrase has it, it has more than one trick up its sleeve. It insisted on entering our realm. Let it stay there.

Whenever I examine it, I do so without bitterness, but

soon turn away. Its enormous eye which stares at me
unseeingly makes me uneasy.)

It seems remarkable to me that this alien poem (alien but
for my substance) tells me its own story and that this angel
makes me tell of him as if I had known him a long time, in
the first person. Which proves that without the vehicle of me
this personality was not prone to assume concrete form and
that, just like the djinns of oriental fables, he could not but
inhabit the vessel of my body. The only way in which an
abstraction can become concrete and still remain invisible is
by marriage with human flesh, reserving for itself the major
part, conceding us only an infinitesimal element of visibility.
And that, of course, all disapproval.

\*          \*          \*

Delivered, emptied, rather weak, I settled in at Villefranche. I had just made it up with Stravinsky in a sleeping-
car where we happened to find ourselves travelling together.
We washed our linen, very dry and stiff too, since *le Coq et
l'Arlequin*. He then asked me to write the text of an oratorio
to be entitled *Oedipus Rex*.

Stravinsky had so far Latinised himself that he wanted
this oratorio to be in Latin. In that task of production,
reminiscent of school, the Revd Father Daniélou was my
assistant.

Stravinsky lived at Mont Boron with his wife and son. I
recall a wonderful joint trip into the mountains. February
was draping the heights in pink summits of trees. Stravinsky
had brought his son Theodore with us. Our driver was
oracular, speaking always with one finger erect. We nick-
named him Tiresias.

It was during this season that I wrote *Orpheus*. In Septem-
ber 1925 I read it at the Mont Boron villa. Stravinsky was
then re orchestrating *le Sacre du Printemps* and composing the
music for *Oedipus Rex*, which he said had to be curly, like
Zeus's beard.

D

I took the text to him as Daniélou and I finished it. I was young. There was sunshine, fishing, regattas. After working I would walk back through the night, fatigueless, all the way to Villefranche. Heurtebise left me in peace. He was now but a stage angel.

Nevertheless, in *Opium* I have noted curious and interesting coincidences which accompanied the Pitoeff production in June, 1926, coincidences which linked up and became serious in Mexico. Again quoting from *Opium*: "*Orpheus* was played in Spanish in Mexico. An earthquake interrupted the Bacchantes scene, destroying the theatre and injuring a number of people. When the damage was repaired, they put the thing on again. All at once, a producer announced that they would have to break off the performance. The actor playing the part of Orpheus could not get out of the mirror. He had died in the wings."

\*        \*        \*

The play, written in 1925, was to have its first performance in 1926, when I got back from a holiday. The second reading took place at Jean Hugo's in Lamballe Avenue. After the reading in the hall, I heard Paul Morand, drawing on his coat, babbling away. "You've opened a funny door there," he said. "That funny door of yours isn't funny either. Not funny at all."

The following day, I lunched at Picasso's in la Boétie Street. There I was again in that lift. I looked at the switchboard. But—the maker's name was now *Otis-Pifre*. Heurtebise had vanished.

\*        \*        \*

P.S. Regarding haunting and malice (crockery breaking, stones falling) which in some houses seem to be the work of some mysterious and very stupid force, one should glance at Emile Tizané's remarkable book: *Sur la Piste de l'Homme inconnu*. A first study, with sound evidence, on these little still unexplained phenomena which engage us.

What does Picasso do if not to transplace objects from one meaning to another—and to break crockery? But his haunted house gets through without police enquiry. It only stirs up the art critics.

For that matter, these phenomena lost much of their mystery at the *Exhibition of Domestic Arts* of 1952. A cake plate there would rise from the table, move around and set itself down before each guest. True, that flying plate attracted the crowd less than the cakes it bore. Only a child was afraid of it and dared not touch it, though he in fact might have been the motive force.

These phenomena are often at the root of the process ascribed to poets. At Joan of Arc's trial, the staff general hid behind a bishop who, rejecting the notion of a miracle, accredited the phenomena to haunting and occult forces. Joan is the victim more of that than of any trap set by foreign politics.

The minor phenomena which Tizané tells of are to give rise to countless enquiries and also to unjust punishments, even to murder in the countryside. The culprit is not discovered, for he expresses himself through many and without their knowledge. Men all suspect each other and, being afraid of laying the charge against something, they ease their minds by laying it against some poor individual.

# Of the Innocence of Criminals

> I would rather you had pleaded guilty.
> One knows how to take a guilty man.
> The innocent elude us and do but
> engender anarchy.
>
> First version of the scene of the
> Cardinal and Hans, in Act 2 of *Bacchus*.

*Chairman of Bench:* You are charged with not being the culprit.
Do you plead guilty?
*Defendant:* I plead guilty.
*Chairman:* Have you committed any precise crime which falls
under the law?
*Defendant:* I have never done anything right.
*Chairman:* That does not improve your case. We do not judge good
here. Good has nothing to do with justice. Only wrong counts in
the eyes of the law. And even that, I repeat, only if it takes a
precise form. Now, on your own admission you have done wrong,
vaguely, which is no excuse. Don't boast! We have witnesses and
proofs. Have you killed? Stolen? Seduced?
*Defendant:* No, but . . .
*Chairman:* That's just it.

*Court Gazette.*

DURING the evacuation, in 1940, at Aix, I knew a
young couple who were closely connected with a
family which sheltered me. It was a medical atmosphere. Dr. M., in whose house I spent this period, lived in
town. Dr. F. and his young wife lived in a little house on the
main road. Behind it a strip of orchards and kitchen gardens
bordered on open country. This little house had belonged to
the young woman's parents. They had inherited it from
theirs, who had inherited in the same way. It all went back
so far that in our quicksand age the very house served as
symbol of rare continuity.

Being neighbourly, we saw a lot of each other and often dined with each other.

The young wife roused my curiosity. At the least breath of wind her beauty and gaiety faded quite out. A little later, she would recover just as quickly. One might have said that she suddenly sighted a menacing wave, when it was still far off, a wave she feared, and tried to prevent its approach. In such moments her features were those of somebody hunted, both expression and gestures suggested somebody under some quite definite threat. She neither heard what was said or responded. She aged, so visibly that her husband could not take his eyes off her, and we imitated his silence. The discomfort would become unbearable. We had to wait till the wave became a reality, overwhelming its victim, at last to break and disappear again.

Such crises were terminated by the inverse process. Then the young woman became all charm, her husband smiled again, conversation revived. The discomfiture gave place to cheerful mood, as if there never had been anything abnormal.

One day, when I was discussing our young friends with Dr. M., I asked him if the wife was neurotic, or if he knew of any shock in her past which might be the cause and origin of those symptoms. Whether, for instance, she had been the victim of some violence, whether an old fear were not at the basis of her condition.

The doctor replied that he thought this was the case, but that the only story of which he had knowledge seemed to him very remote and not very conclusive. But of course, he added, anything was possible. We did not know very much what went on in the catacombs of the human body. The case really called for a psycho-analyst.

Now, for reasons which you will appreciate, Mme. F. refused to subject herself to analysis. Add to her condition the fact that she had no children, and that the mere thought of another pregnancy threw her into fits of horror which did not improve her disorder.

Here is the story of that early shock which the doctor told me.

Our young friend was an only child. Her father and mother gave way to her every caprice. She had just turned five when her mother again became pregnant. The confinement was at hand and they felt they had to tell the little girl that they were expecting a brother or a sister to arrive for her.

As everybody knows, it is, alas, customary to trick children, confusing them with fairy-tales about their own birth. I find such fairy-tales ridiculous. My children know that they come from their mother's belly. They do not love her any the less for that knowledge, and we avoid the danger they may make grim discoveries, seeking out the truth from each other at school. In short, the little girl who concerns us lived in lies, and that was the origin of the tragedies which followed.

The father and mother wondered how to prepare this little girl, already so jealous of her rights, for the sudden incursion of a boy or girl intruder and the need to share her universe with him or her, for the child drove her dominion to the point of rejecting all the dogs and cats offered to her, afraid lest her parents took a liking to them and thereby deprived her of some little portion of their love for her.

So, with a thousand precautions, they told her that "Heaven" was sending them a little boy or a little girl, that the news about it was not quite definite as to which it would be, but that the date was fixed, also that she should be pleased, as they were, at this wonderful news, and almost certainly the Heavenly present would reach them in a couple of days time.

They had feared tears, but they were surprised. The child did not cry at all. But her eyes turned to ice. Instead of crying she now frightened them by the grim silence of a grown woman informed by her lawyer that she had lost all her worldly wealth.

Nothing is more incorruptible than the seriousness of

childhood when it is stubborn. In vain the parents kissed and petted, smothering the information with kind words, in face of that dead-pan reception all their little tricks became ridiculous.

Right up to the confinement, the little girl offered the same stony expression to all attempts to touch her heart. At last, the actual confinement preoccupied the parents, leaving the child free to shut herself up in her room and gnaw into her own bitterness.

The young wife now gave birth—to a stillborn child. Her husband tried to console her by saying that at least this would make it easier for their little daughter. If they told her that at the last resort they had declined the present, because it hurt her, she would recover her interest in life

The device failed. Not merely did the child not change her attitude. She made things worse by falling ill. Temperature and delirium gave a clinical picture of inflammation of the lungs. Dr. M. thought somebody must have been very careless for the child to catch such a chill, but Dr. F. could not think how it could have happened. However, he now told his colleague all about the child's emotional upset. But Dr. M. insisted that though this could have given rise to a nervous trouble, it did not explain away a lung inflammation, for which the standard treatment would have to be prescribed. The child's life was saved, but when all this was over, things really did become puzzling. No tenderness seemed able to break through the child's iciness. Convalescent, she was clearly eating her heart out. The acute illness was followed by another which was quite mysterious.

It was then that Dr. M., despairing of finding what was wrong, suggested psycho-analysis, for, he said, a psycho-analyst would have the courage to venture into a realm on the borders of which the positive science of our time hesitates, confessing its impotence. "Professor H. is my nephew," he said. "He must be made yours too. At least, let the child think so. Then he could come and stay with you. I know him well enough to be confident that he will agree to such artifice."

It so happened that the psycho-analyst was about to take his holidays, and did consent to spend them at Aix, "with his uncle". Every day he spent with the young family, enquiring into things and becoming their friend. The little girl was suspicious of him, but gradually even she became inured to him. She even seemed rather flattered by the attentions of a grown-up who did not treat her like a little silly, but as an equal. And she called him *Uncle*.

After a month of this, she became talkative and he could chatter with her. One day, they were together at the bottom of the garden, well away from the parents and the servants. And then, without a word of warning and as unruffled as any defendant pouring forth a confession to the examining magistrate, she got rid of the secret which in its efforts to escape from the shadows within her must have been choking her.

In place of her actual story, let us relate in our own words what happened.

*      *      *

It was the night of the confinement. The previous day, snow had fallen. The little girl did not sleep. She was on the watch. She knew that in the morning, perhaps at daybreak, the present was to reach their address. She also knew that that sort of present necessitated some kind of domestic ceremonial which was being kept well screened from her. There was not a moment to be lost.

Strong in her knowledge, she got up, without any light, left her room, which was on the first storey, lifted the skirts of her long nightie well off the ground and tiptoed down the stairs. Whenever one creaked, she halted, and could hear her own heart beating. A door opened slightly. She pressed back against the banisters and saw an unknown woman in a cloak and white headdress cross the oblong of light thrown from the open doorway on to the tiles of the hall. The stranger entered the sitting-room which came before her parents' room and shut the door, leaving the first door open. This led into an uncomfortable bathroom and dressing-room, where her mother used to do her hair, powder, pin on hats and veils.

The child continued on her way down, crossed the hall, and slipped into the room which the white stranger had just left. She was dying with fear lest the stranger should come back at once.

On the dressing-table there was a pin-cushion full of hat-pins, which in the period in question were worn very long. She took one with a baroque pearl knob and slipped to the outer door, with its iron work and coloured glass. The door was locked and she had to reach that lock. She was brave enough to find a chair and climb up. She turned the key, got down, put the chair back again.

Once outside, in the porch, she closed the door quietly and peeped through the glass panes, nearly out of reach of her eyes. Just in time. The woman in white was crossing the hall. There was also a gentleman in a morning-coat with her and he was waving his hands. They vanished into the bathroom.

The child did not feel any cold. She went round the corner of the house, and, just as she was, bare-foot, in her nightie, she ran across the empty garden beds. The ground was frozen hard. She could feel nothing in the icy moonlight. The garden was asleep as it stood. Well as she knew it. Every portion of it familiar, it filled her with terrors. It was as still as armed sentinels, behind every single tree there was a man hidden. The mere sight of it all made her feel that something terrible was about to happen.

Of course, the child was not conscious of the transformation. All she knew was that her dear garden thus full of linen on the line, of unknown horrors, of graves, was unrecognisable.

She ran. She held up her nightie and clutched her hat-pin. It seemed she would never get there. Her destination lay at the far end of the garden, precisely where, in fact, she now told the professor in her own language all these details which subsequently he told me. No doubt, as often happens, it was the scene of the crime which prompted the confession.

For she halted at last. Yes, this was the kitchen garden. She was burning and shivering too. The moon did not turn the cabbages into anything more terrible than what they were. To the child the terrible thing in fact about them was precisely that they were cabbages. They were unmistakable, hard outlines, magnified in the moonlight. She bent down and, without hesitation, just sticking her tongue out a bit like an attentive schoolchild, poked at the first cabbage with her pin. The cabbage resisted and squeaked. So she pulled out the pin, seized the pearly knob more firmly and stabbed hard. One cabbage after another she stabbed, furiously. The pin began to twist. She grew calmer, then more steadily and more carefully completed her work.

She stuck that hat-pin's point into the very heart of the leaves of every cabbage, where they curled back, and she leant on it with all her strength, driving the pin home to the hilt. In some cases the pin would not come out of the wound. She had to pull with both hands, and she fell backwards more than once. But nothing discouraged her. Her greatest fear was to leave out a cabbage.

Her task done, the little murderess inspected her victims. She was like Ali-Baba's servant going round the jars of oil, to make sure none of them had escaped massacre.

When she went back indoors, she no longer ran. Nor was she any more afraid of the garden. It had become her accomplice. Without realising the process, she was given new courage by the new, criminal aspect of the place. It supported her, with a kind of triumph She was in the highest of spirits.

Nor was she aware of any dangers when she came back. She climbed the railing, opened the door, closed it again, moved the chair once more, then put it back, stuck the pin back into the pin-cushion, crossed the hall, went upstairs, got back to her room, and into bed, and her peace of mind was so great that she fell asleep at once.

\*         \*         \*

The psychiatrist contemplated the cabbage-patch, imagining the astonishing scene.

"I stabbed them all, all of them!" the little girl said. "I stabbed them all, then I went back indoors."

And the psychiatrist was able to reconstruct the crime which I relate.

"I went back indoors. I was very pleased. I slept very well."

She slept well, but when she woke up she had a temperature of 104° F.

\*         \*         \*

The Professor was then able to explain to the young couple that when they had told the child that it was after all better for them to have only her, she did not believe what they said, because she knew she was guilty, it was not her parents who refused the little brother or sister, it was she who had killed it. Of that she was quite sure. And she was eaten up with remorse. It ate deep into her.

"You," the psychiatrist said, "will now have to prove to her the real truth—for I have made no attempt to do it—that children are not really born in the garden in cabbages. I hope you see now what horrors such idiotic stories can lead to."

\*         \*         \*

Doctor M. added that the parents consented most unwillingly to follow this advice. They believed the truth to be a sacrilege committed against their own childhood! They live now at Marseilles. When they stay at Aix, they still profess to be puzzled by their daughter's nervous tension and her anxiety about her constant miscarriages!

And you, I said to Dr. M., would say that this old story was the root cause?

"I affirm nothing," he replied, "but I do recall that it was when the child was fifteen that her parents, called away on business, brought her to stay with me. My nephew came at the time to spend a week with me. She was then quite a big girl, and as well as the truth that babies are not found in cabbages, she also knew that the Professor was not really a member of her family, but of ours, and all the story about being an uncle was humbug.

"One evening we were unwise enough to start delving in the past.

" 'Do you know the real tragedy of that cabbage business?' asked my nephew. 'The real truth, you know, is that she did in fact commit that murder. Instinctively the child made use, and successfully too, of all the procedure of sympathetic magic. And sympathetic magic is not funny at all.'

"We proceeded to discuss sympathetic magic, and ended up by recognising that it was a proved thing.

" 'It is not impossible,' was my own conclusion. 'You may be right, she did murder. No matter, so long as she never suspects it'."

Later, however the doctor told me that he and his wife discovered that the young hussy was good at eavesdropping.

\*        \*        \*

P.S. A Freudian Family: Mrs. X. enters the room. Her nine-year-old daughter is drawing with a red pencil. Nanny is at church. Mrs. X. bends down to peep. What is her little pettie drawing? It is a huge phallus!

Taking precious little notice of her child's screams, Mrs. X. snatches away the paper and disappears. Mr. X. comes home from his golf.

"Just you look at this," cries Mrs. X.

Mr. X. nearly has a fit.

"Now where can that unhappy child have seen anything like that?" asks Mrs. X.

"That's just what I should like to know," says Mr. X.

We can leave out the investigation. After four days of it, Monsieur again interrogates his daughter. And at last he gets the answer.

"But, daddy, that was only a drawing of Nanny's scissors."

# On the Death Penalty

I AM more shy of feelings than acts and whereas in itself nonconformity of deed rarely upsets me, on the other hand I do find it unpleasant to have all a man's backroom stock brought out. I should never be ashamed by exhibition of externals, but exhibition of intimate things does shock me. In addition, I find it very dubious.

That is why this Ledger is not really one.

I should find it very nearly just if the law offered its protection to those scandals which we see but prevented the revelation of those invisible. These however are not envisaged by the code. (I am of course not referring here to the Baudelaire, Flaubert and similar court cases, the texts of which contain nothing scandalous. The scandalous in my judgment being lies labelled confessions.) None the less, wise caution lends poets that masking style in which they conceal the shamelessness of their souls, and what outrages me in reading the daily press is not the parade of thefts and murders, but what prompted such murders or thefts—and the investigations which cluster round them. I have the impression that the guilty are no longer prosecuted in town or country but in a darkness in which it must be most difficult to distinguish between prosecuted and prosecuting.

One lot lie, delighting in exhibitionism (as we see clearly from the cases of innocent persons gushing out false confessions) while the other lot bark in unison, endowing with their own well-concealed impulses the person interrogated. This is of course all but a revelling in self-accusation minus the risk. It is self-flagellation minus the pain that prompts press and public to feed so gluttonously on horrors.

With a good crime, the sale of the daily papers trebles. Intrigues in which decked out as humanity struts hypocrisy are endlessly dragged out. Hereby public and the protagonists of crime merge. As if one dreamt them all on biers.*

In the trial of Loeb and Leopold, which was the prototype of intellectual crime of which Hitchcock's film *The Rope* was to be the high point, the defendant's counsel, having asserted that every man bore within himself an occult desire to murder, and testily asked by the prosecutor how he dared impute to the court such a desire, saved the two culprits from the electric chair by asking dramatically whether it was then not true that for several weeks now the prosecution had been trying to accomplish the violent wilful death of Loeb and Leopold.

Man merely follows the rhythm of plants and animals which devour each other, but does so under a system of law which leads all the way up to legal murder. This, never having the excuse of a psychotic impulse when it kills, is reminiscent of the brothel, in which sex goes through its motions coldly, unprovoked by real love.

The death penalty is untenable. Massacre is the real law. If we pile precise laws on such law as this, all imprecision, we merely become artificial and condemn ourselves in others. Judges and juries should analyse their own motives as seriously as they strive to master and corner the stag. Let them raise the havoc of riot in themselves. They would then probably regret their verdicts, unless they found pride in being their own hunting-ground and were also able to call the hunt off before the kill.

*     *     *

At the Nuremberg trial those who climbed high in judgment over others were themselves the judged. High starched

---

* *After the Lurs murder, the police even had forcibly to chase away people who wanted to picnic on "the very spots" where the murders were committed.*

collars are no protection against the rope. Really, immediate revenge would have been preferable. With such immediate justice a court is relieved from punishing what it respects above all in the world: discipline and obedience to orders from above.

*       *       *

As far as I myself go, it would be braggart of me to claim no responsibility on the grounds that I am incapable of killing a fly, for I eat the cattle whose sufferings in the slaughter-house I could never bear. And have I not on occasion secretly nursed dreams of wreaking a justice (my own) which would make mincemeat of my enemies?

Men were quick to charge those who submitted to a dictatorship. But one can count on one's fingers those who would disobey gruesome orders in the knowledge that their disobedience would result in their own destruction. From a distance one can see that such brave rebellion is rare. It is incumbent on us to salute the patriots who did invalidate this law in the chambers of the Gestapo. Among others, Jean Desbordes, a man who could not bear to see a street accident but died under torture rather than tell.

*       *       *

The prestige of bloodshed is peculiar. One would think it was a lava of our inner fire seeking self-recognition in it. The sight of blood disgusts me. But that did not prevent me calling a film *A Poet's Blood* and in that film several times showing blood-shed—or the Oedipus story which I have tackled several times being well stained with blood.

One might say that we find our revenge against the defences of the invisible by trying to surprise the springs of scarlet bubbling up in that realm. One would say that we have transferred the mystery of bloodshed of the savage to our cerebral sphere, a mystery so powerful that there are islands where the natives cut each other's throats all day, junket together all night, and resume throat-slitting the next day.

This mysteriousness of our motives however assumes a troublesome aspect when it begins to act under the grand sign of the sword of justice, when it surrounds itself with pomp, providing a spectacle for the masses who delight thus gratis to satisfy their primitive urges.

One of the most worrying forms which hypocrisy takes, quite apart from its readiness to come down on vices in which itself it secretly indulges, is the extremity to which the shame of lying drives the hypocrite, compelling him to offer up his blushes as flushes of indignation.

*I must kill my brother.* That is what the culprit at liberty thinks when he has before him the captured culprit. Perhaps this reflex satisfies the need which cowardly men have of punishing themselves in the form of another.

It will be argued against me that monsters must be suppressed. But when all is said and done it still astonishes me that people can bolster themselves up with chatter about supreme justice when every minute that supreme justice makes it most manifest to us that it is administered according to a code which is incomprehensible, one which baffles our own kind, represses the good people, is accommodating to the bad, doubtless enough all in the name of an economy, but one which is hidden from us and never requires them to assume the victim's place themselves.

Nature drives us to mass destruction. That destructive madness promotes its own forms of imbalance, its differences of level, those avalanches of blind force which feed the machine. But I find it hard to believe that a criminal or an assize court offer Nature satisfactory aid, for Nature's own progression is by vast waves, on crude pretexts, with cataclysmic rectifications of any errors of judgment.

\*      \*      \*

Being drawn by lot as juryman would for me be prime ill luck. Whatever can we do around a table at which we should prefer the guests not to be our hosts? Besides, confronted with

E

our doubts, would there not inevitably be among us one of those robust fellows who boast of their prowess at carving the joint? But on our dish is a defendant, and his is the skin we might propose to carve. Not that of our robust member, who for his greater gastronomic vainglory would like to lead us to a cannibal feast.

What *modest* pride one sees sparkle in the very bearing of a jury as it files back into court after its deliberations! What distress in the bearing of the misfortunate whose single voice has not enjoyed much credit!

The discomfiture which one finds when confronted with such spectacles has profound causes which it would be well for us to study a little. The Muscovian *ukaz* never envisaged radio or cinema, nor the Napoleonic Code psychiatry. You may say that psychiatrists are consulted. None the less, the verdict is dependent on the mood and the circumstances, which swing those guests to right or left, and on whether their belly happens to be replete or is starving and deaf. Round that table what is principally lacking is the belly with a heart in it.

*          *          *

Re-reading G. M. Gilbert's book on the back-room work of the Nuremberg trial (I mean his *Nuremberg Diary*) one is staggered by the utter infantilism of that band of men who upset the whole world. We tend to credit them with vision matching our own misfortunes. We imagine the members of the whole gang to have been linked together with the seriousness of criminologists and by profound political motives. Differences of rank no longer partition off their relationships. They delight in the figure test and the finger-print tests inflicted on them. They deflate. They become voluble. And what do we behold, but petty jealousies and idiotic feuds. Cads and hooligans of the lower-fifth amusing themselves. Monstrous schoolboy practical jokes invented at Auschwitz, Colonel Hoess, the death of two and a half million

Jews led to believe they were being taken to the shower-baths, tricked by sham railway stations or trick halts at the doors to gas-chambers. And those *No, sir, not me, sir,* with every one of them trying to pass responsibility to some other one. All of which goes to bear out my theory about the terrifying irresponsibility of responsible figures, about that braggadocio of responsibility on which Chateaubriand's words about Napoleon in a runaway coach kidding himself that he was driving throws light.

Bergson would explain that their fall turns these captains and ministers and men of diplomacy into puppets. Bergson's followers, on the contrary, would say that their fall de-puppetizes them and reveals them as they really are. But the ludicrousness of such falls is certainly no laughing-matter.

\*           \*           \*

Eddington writes that events do not reach us, we come upon them *en passant.*

One should realise that these fixed events do not belong to our three dimensions. Their facets are multiple. They may be approached from any one of many angles of their multiformity. Free choice and fatalism inter-tangle. For one tends to fit in with what hazard brings by the pretext that it offers us only one aspect. But in fact it possesses several, contradictory one to another, too, with a scheme of tenses like the double-facedness of Janus.

It must be belief that fate (just like ourselves) has only one face that comforts jurymen after a verdict of death. *Thus was it written.* Perhaps, if that is so, they should have read what was written in a mirror, which would provide some surprises. It would also offer the wonderful good fortune of seeing at the same time both man and his reflection, the two sides of the barrier.

What does a painter do to detect the errors in the portrait he is painting? He looks at it in a mirror. When he returns home in the evening the juryman sees himself in the glass, and the glass reverses him, brings out the errors of his head. And the head pleads: "Ought we not to have been critics? Proved our perspicacity? Shown no credulity? Not let ourselves be persuaded by the defending counsel's rhetoric? Should we not have given justice a surprise with our own? Should we have given way to that court captivated by play-actors?"

\*　　　\*　　　\*

If I am reproached (otherwise congratulated) with having signed so many appeals for mercy, particularly those of my opponents, let me say that I did not sign them out of greatness of heart, but because in my mirror I refuse to see a head which the reflecting, reversing surface could charge with the crime of responsibility.

After all, what part does your inexorable jury play? To ruin the play? But we are not in the theatre. The red curtain is the knife of the guillotine—or the hangman's rope.

\*　　　\*　　　\*

The moment legality ceases to function and it comes to the people making their own laws, or when such blunders as that of the *Champ de Mars* give men a free hand, one gets back to primitive blood law. There is no saving the man seized and torn to pieces by the crowd. He is run through or roped up. In vain do the ideologists of revolution spar about, trying to persuade the crowd to wait till "justice" can be done. Everywhere then quite another justice functions. Besides, there is no possible proof that if a victim did escape his illegal executioners, these ideologists' "proper" justice would not bring him to the hands of the legal executioner by a much slower, more painful road.

An ideology has roots like those of popular reflexes, and therein lies its great value. But it wraps itself up in legalities and even when it seeks to pardon, its fear of losing its direction and alienating the crowd persuades it to approve of crowd justice.

Only time soothes such fevers. One then sees a relaxation, a fatigue, in which the machinery runs in reverse. An after-dinner nap saves those condemned men who have had the fortune to live in prison. In fact what they are doing is taking advantage of the ogre's digestive processes. The smallest of victims now would turn his stomach.

One thing is clear, justice cannot be objective. A court groups individuals by subjective reactions. And if it is sad to see a studious pupil ploughed by one vote, it is grim indeed if, when there is doubt in a case, one single vote against can send a defendant to the guillotine.*

One evening, when a cinema was showing a film by Cay-atten on this subject, I watched people's expressions during the showing and as they went out. During, the argument seemed to be convincing them. But when they emerged from the darkened hall they woke up from their collective hypnosis and reassumed the features of the cannibal gentlemen of the jury. Each individual slipped back into pride in those titles to nobility which responsibility confers  Most likely any person whatsoever in that audience would in his pride at receiving an official summons to serve forget all about the film and say to himself: duty first. From that instant the life of any defendant would hang by a mere thread.

Nevertheless, I do observe that even if the notion of war as subject to the secret designs of Nature finds countless adherents, that of the death penalty does today find more and more objectors. Pamphlets and petition forms are going the rounds. And just as youth labours all out and seems bent

* *The French jury works by a majority vote; the English jury requires unanimity. When all the jurymen are robust of ethic, this is a safeguard. With the typical yes-men of modern "highly civilised" mankind on juries, as in Britain, the unanimity becomes merely that of a totalitarian election, the two systems are thus identical, and the English one is merely the majority savagery of the French one camouflaged with typical English humbug.—* Translator.

on breaking the sound barrier, that is to say, the silence barrier, so likewise countless individuals are working together to spread the ideals of anti-racism and to oppose the death penalty.

How such movements serve or disserve the cold calculations of Nature, I cannot say. That is a state of disorder in which man takes part without, alas, being able to introduce any order. The order of one not being the order of the other, and Nature leaving us free only to the extent to which our efforts do not introduce order into the disorder which she maintains as her own system of order.

# On a Piece of Gallantry

THE divorce between religion and science is a great mistake. A sort of ricochet of the original one. We all bear the weight of that error of the 19th century. We are responsible for it. Science is responsible for not having grasped that the symbols of religion concealed numbers. Religion is responsible for forgetting the key to the numbers while clinging to their symbols.

And all that pride of science, just to get back to Heraclitus, to the triad, the triangle, the trinity, of which the Father, Son and Holy Ghost, represented by a patriarch, a young man and a bird, are merely the conventional signs, designed for the simple.

Many great scientists of our day are believers, and religion is drawing closer, catching up with science. A great pity it does this, when it might hold it back.

\*         \*         \*

The more science bangs its head against the figure 3 and the figure 7 (which sum up the triad and those four feet which the 19th century planted on such solid ground), the more it respects 0, and the more the figure 1 astonishes it.

For though man by disintegrating matter does dismember the figure 3, he does so but only in trifling amounts, and then merely to destroy other men's figure 4, so that his own may be cock of the walk. To the 0 he restores this 4 of other people, without grasping that the figure 3—which enters into everything—is re-forming right under his nose or his beard, and also that those 4's, of power still unknown, will re-form and some day be a menace to him.

Those tall vast pillars of fire which rose from Hiroshima and Nagasaki were but the rage of the figure 3, reintegrating and coming back, in a zone where man no longer meddles in what does not concern him.

Let us listen to the words of one of the pilots of the super-fortress named *Great Artist* after he had dropped the bomb: *I am not so sure that we were not playing with forces which did not concern us.* Fateful play, up to the moment when, its patience exhausted by human silliness, silliness which men persist in thinking genius, the figure 1 will drive them to play a bit too much with that triad and they will reduce our poor world to the zero out of which it arose.

\*          \*          \*

Centuries have been necessary for man to get clear about the certainty that space and time are functions one of another. Yet it seems so elementary to observe that the time which separates us from a house diminishes proportionately and inversely to the size of the house as it grows larger and that the house does not achieve habitable volume in space till the gap of time which allows us to reach it is no longer inhabited by us. There is an exchange of dwellings. One would be impossible without the other. Indeed, from far off man resorts to strange acrobatics to be able to recognise a house so minute and imagine what it may contain.

Should I repeat it: in man's mind the perspective of time dissociated from space serves as a sort of inside-out space where things get smaller when removed to a distance, whereas when time removes them from us they tend to grow larger. It is this that distorts the incidents of childhood—and historical events. They assume enormous proportions owing to this amplification factor.

\*          \*          \*

Time and space together form so elastic and so outrageous an amalgam that man is constantly finding himself faced with little proofs that he really tends to get lost in it all, knowing it in fact very badly indeed. For instance, when in our films, in an interior scene, an actor opens a door of a house which opens outwards, then in the studio some weeks later closes the "same" door on the inside the screen finally shows it all as if part of the same action. The film montage obliterates the intervening time in which the actor lived his own life, and represents this man as living very differently from what he thinks. It is true, of course, that the space and time blocks which the film producer cuts out and sticks together again are keyed integrally to each other, but the point is—can we be sure that the amalgam of time and space thus fabricated is really artificial at all? I sometimes wonder. Employing it, we certainly find reality. Many cases of false witness, too, derive from a similar mechanism, as when a juryman is cheated by the distorting perspectives of space and time and with complete good faith decides on the death of his brother.

*          *          *

There are documentary films which when they show us the world of plants, by speeding up the succession of images rub our noses in our own dirt because of the slow motion which results.

When these frames are turned at normal speed, the film is proof that the vegetable world lives a very stormy, grim, erotic, cruel life. A great difference between its beat and ours makes that life invisible to us, giving us an illusory view of the vegetable world, in particular regarding its supposed serenity. Which leads us to conclude that all that we believe solid, stable, inert, is really teeming with life, all fermentation, and that a ciné-camera equipped with unbelievably fast shutter speeds would reveal solid matter itself to be nothing but savage matings, occult vices, opposites devouring each other, wild tornadoes of gravitation.

The first time that Germany sent us its films based on differences of speed of turning, applied to the vegetable kingdom, the French censorship got frightened, considering (and rightly, too) that the films were like those of Marseilles brothels. The films were in fact prohibited. We saw them in secret. There was no question about the resemblance. Adhesive mucosities, phalloi, vulvae, sperm and spasm filled the screen.

The runner haricot bean offered a less flagrantly obscene interlude, as it wound its way up its pole. One would have said it was licking it, like a cat licking its paws. It might have been a young monkey, or a gnome, agile and harmless. But while I was marvelling at its restlessness and its charm, an elderly lady ejaculated to the darkened hall: "Good Heavens! I shall never eat those horrid beans again." Grand old lady, she will before long be put to earth herself and eventually help beans of some sort to grow.

\*      \*      \*

All this would be funny, were it not sad. And one certainly gets the impression that the more man studies, the more he researches till he thinks he has got to the heart of the mystery, the farther from it all he is, because he is in fact constantly slithering down a mountain of errors, and even when he thinks he really is climbing back towards the top, he has no choice, he is still slithering down, lower and lower.

That is why religion once restrained science and kept it secret. Religion only made use of science to impress the masses and keep them respectful. The moment the crowd meddles you have confusion. And the censorship which at the time I condemned was perhaps wise not to complicate the teachings of Sigmund Freud by exposing the intimacies of flowers and vegetables.

Great wisdom was there in the counsel guiding the Israelites when they had to deposit a copy of their books in the hands of authority, substituting a cypher and masking their social, economic and scientific discoveries in fables. These fables became the creed of a Church which in the sixteenth century suspected them, without guessing that they were the inverse of what they seemed to be when read. That lost cypher should be the subject of keen study, having surely given rise to misunderstandings, some even carried over by the translators of the translation (Luther's abounds in them) demanding profound knowledge of Hebrew, of the double and triple meanings of that tongue. I should never have suspected anything of this had Mme. Bessonet-Fabre not long since enlightened me regarding this cypher and given me her commentary on certain parables, which then lost their obscure charm and became astoundingly translucid.

Those fables are durable. They were the staple of superficial catholicism. Such catholicism rises up against the Pope when he accepts them as fables and is filled with anxiety about what is hidden beneath the cypher.

But when in 1952 the Pope made a declaration regarding the relations between religion and science, the divorce persisted and that was a pity. For it prevented priests recovering their original privileges, so preaching the gospel in the centre of a triangle in which are inscribed a heart and an eye.

One would thus have gleaned what Christ was suggesting in the words: *In the house of my father there are many habitations*, and one would have realised that all religions are but one, that the meaning of the cyphers changes, but that they all add up to the same sum.

And as earthly mechanics cannot do aught but follow the mechanics of the universe, one would get a viable Europe, a land, how should I put it, in which men would respect the cyphers which direct them and leave to Nature the responsibility of providing the inequalities (changing its levels about). Nature moreover would cope, she would produce her Augean washing-days, by the grace of epidemics, earthquakes, cyclones, tidal waves, car accidents, air smashes, suicides, natural deaths and other bags of ballast to be thrown out and provide the daily newspapers with "stories". (The *Journal* of today, March 5th, 1952, for instance, tells me about the following: Tragic Accident on Nice-Paris Express; North Japan Ravaged by Earthquake followed by Tidal-Wave; Railway Accident in Brazil; Small Pox in Marseilles; Arkansas, Alabama and Georgia Ravaged by Tornado; More Deaths on U.S.A. Roads than in Korea—and so on and so forth).

But I digress. It may be by man's inability to admit the tenets of others, and his persistence in imposing his own that he assists Nature's imbalances. Thereby from our disobedient species Nature obtains the martial bent which without trouble she imposes on peaceable reigns. Thus man imagines he is the victim of a series of wars, and fails to grasp that there is merely one war, within which there are rest intervals which he takes to be "peace".

*          *          *

Let us not fly away from our subject, this conflict between the visible and the invisible, the enquiry into which is trying to lead us too far afield. The more so since the above is the logical prologue to a very characteristic adventure in which the fables which clothe the cypher serve as excuses to powers which wish me invisible, and hide away my cypher under shockingly visible shapes.

*          *          *

As I was completing my play *Bacchus* I had a presentiment that something was about to happen, but could not guess what. Laughing, I even remarked to Mme. W., in whose hospitable house I was working: "Reinforce your vessel, for we shall have to take flight."

I ought to have known clearly from an event which seemed funny, but in which one cannot but perceive the medieval style of our age.

At Dijon an effigy of Father Christmas had just been publicly burned, the Church accusing him of being a dangerous German custom calculated to lead children astray. If the poor kiddies believe that fable, they deserve burning alive themselves as heretics.

In short, I foresaw an imperialist attack on *Bacchus* on the lines of "*You are embarrassing me, I shall kill you.*" But I was unable to foresee from what direction the actual attack would come, from what window they would start sniping, for my play offered a number of targets. But anyway, since my stage play is extremely visible, it was up to the invisible to rally its defence arsenal.

Most unexpectedly, for he is an old friend of mine, the gunman was François Mauriac. We had made our first essays at shooting together and it would have seemed unthinkable to me for him to turn any of his guns against me.

The attack was directed by an imperialist power: that of Literature with capital "L", though of course, cloaked and daggered as: *Morals*!

The sniper's imprudence was, shortly before this, to have published (in the *la Table Ronde*) an article in which he stood up for the free expression of the artist and his right to say *everything*. The only snag was that Mauriac stood up for that right to suit Mauriac.

As you will see, my good marksman was of that ilk who are slow to level their sights—the confraternity of whom I speak in my *le Secret Professionel*. And he did not even score an outer, because his principal thought was to assume the posture which shows him to best advantage, for he thought the patron saint of snipers was watching.*

* *That external style, separated, as it were, from its subject, that laying on of the paint which obliterates the subject and prompts remarks like "I don't at all share Mauriac's ideas, but how beautifully he does express them"— all of which entirely fails to come off when the style denounces an ethic losing all its decorative qualities, unlikely to attract the insects to whom the ethic remains alien. Then human insects assume that "it is not written". They turn from real flowers, to gorge on artificial blossoms.*

As far as dogma went, I was safe. I had consulted Dominican and Benedictine authorities. I held their *exeatur*. Father Christmas's pyre and Mauriac's deposition of the first faggot for mine were like acts which risk making the beast of the Book of Revelation look quite kindly. Leading minds of the priesthood disapprove of such enterprises. The bishops of Michel de Ghelderode and Sartre do not trouble our lay judges. The arrow misses its target. As preamble to mysticism (mysticism in the wild state), the sacrilege tends to reassure them. Arthur Rimbaud will be made to feel the advantage of that.

*          *          *

I must be a better christian than I am a catholic. *Bacchus* must be a christian play. Cardinal Zampi at heart must be more christian than orthodox.

I do confess to the Vatican's having been shocked by the vine-leaves on the statuary.* On the other hand, I would have found it normal were they to conceal the jewels of the Vatican treasury under vine-leaves. To my mind came Maurras's words, quoted by Gide: "I am not going to leave this learned procession of Fathers, Councils, Popes, all the great men of the modern élite, to tie myself down to the gospels of four obscure Jews." Antisemitism could not go further.

As usual, I am patently on the wrong side of the barricades. And I think of Gide's creed: "I permit nothing to harm me, on the contrary, I want everything to be of some use, I aim at turning everything to my advantage."

That is the creed of visibility. To get the creed of invisibility (mine) you only have to negative these words and add the

---

* Dr. M. had just told me the story of how a certain lady explained to her little girl that she forbade her to look at her little brother's shameful parts, because they were the cause of all the ills which assail us. Having succeeded in the night in amputating the baby boy's parts with a pair of scissors, the child hurried to waken her mother and bring her the glad tidings. She felt quite heroic, a Judith, in fact, and could not get over her astonishment at her mother's real grief.

following of Heraclitus': "In God's eyes everything is good and just. Men, on the other hand, think of some things as just, of others as unjust."

How am I to help it? That's how my factory works. All I hate is—hatred. Yet I find more excuse for hatred than frivolity. And of that I find much in the sniping of my opponents. I am very nearly certain that if Mauriac were to read my play and re-read his open letter, he would be shamed, and would run to weep on his confessor's shoulder.

\*　　　\*　　　\*

I had for a very long time dreamt of writing that play. It came to me first as play, then as film, finally, as book. I went back to the notion of a play, thinking that the stage formed a better framework for the fable. It was from Ramuz that I got that. At Vevey they still have the Bacchanalian customs at vintage time. It all dates from the Sumerian civilisation.

"There are documents," writes J. Perenne, in his *Ancient Civilisation*, "describing the ceremonies observed at the inauguration of the temple of the god Ningirsu. In their jollifications, the people abandoned themselves to real bacchanalia, the origin of which goes back to ancient agricultural rites. For seven days there was general licence in the town. Civil laws and moral laws were in suspension. All authority ceased to be. A slave replaced the king, disposed of the royal harem, was served at the royal table by the royal servants. Once the feast was over, he was sacrificed to the gods so that they should forgive the town its past faults and grant it great increase. In the temple courts sacred rites were performed which were transmitted to Babylon. Saturnalia and rites alike held throughout the whole of Mesopotamian history. We find Berosus taking part in them in the 3rd century. Even Rome was to see those strange festivals come down from the remote past still celebrated, while christianity was to preserve them in its carnival."

My first version was of a dictatorship. In it, a village idiot became a monster. I soon gave that one up. It was too crude. Besides, it resisted me. I had tackled the theme of the confusion of youth and all the dogmas, sects, and other obstacles put in its path. Though at the mercy both of offers of "good openings" and of its feelings, youth strives to preserve its freedom. Its unregulated freedom slipped through the obstacles, but at last it was crushed by them. Youth could only win by trickery or by seizing power. Youth lacked the skill which the maze required. Youth made a wild bull rush. Its luckless right wing, its courage, its heart, its feelings, ill served it in a society ruled by the meander, one in which meanders criss-crossed and grimly clashed.

Hans is all fire, all flame, and very naive. His play may deceive your bishop or your duke, but not your cardinal. The cardinal hails from Rome and knows his sol-fa. He pretends to be taken in because he is gathering information on the crises of a Germany which he is exploring. The duke and the duke's daughter please him. He guesses what disturbance the Reformation brings to families. *Say nothing irreparable.* That is the counsel he tends the duke, adding—in my first version: *Let Christine feel poorly, since only a fainting fit is capable of reducing your family to silence.* He is thus ancestral to Stendhal's prelates. He knows both how to be subtle and how to be kind. He warns Hans: *You are rushing into the flames like a moth.* It is to save the moth from the burning that he manoeuvres. Incapable of catching it in flight, he does save it from the flames, even after its death. In its final act, the Church reveals its perspicacity. Some catholics saw a lie in the right arrogated to himself by Zampi to remain worthy of his rite and his heart.

*       *       *

When Sartre and I learned that we were both busy on plays which alike took place in sixteenth-century Germany, it was too late for either to change the setting. He was at

Saint Tropez finishing *le Diable et le Bon Dieu* and I at Cap
Ferrat had completed my first act. I was well launched. We
decided we would meet at Antibes. Our plots proved to be
utterly dissimilar. I could go on with mine. Our background
facts, however, being the same, Sartre pointed out to me
books which I added to those by which I had learned to
know Luther. Books came in from all over the place.

The difficulty was to take notes, then shut the bundles of
them away in a cupboard and forget about them, to re-live
their essence through the lips of my characters.

It is old phrases presented from a lively angle which seem
subversive. They are showered against me. It is correct to say
that they fit what is happening this year (1952). But the fit
did not come to me till long after. There were coincidences
of this sort which only became clear to me when the audience
laughed or applauded.

\*       \*       \*

Claudel's *Jeanne au Bûcher* puts me off. The Church is one.
Its greatness is in gathering its forces. When it condemns Joan
of Arc and then turns her into a saint I see one person making
an error, then repenting. Canonising Joan, the Church
courageously charges itself with guilt. It is the nobility of that
admission and the come-back against itself that I admire here
in the Church. Were it about Captain Dreyfus and not Saint
Joan, the revision of the Rennes trial would never enable a
dramatist to scoff at the General Staff. Unless of course he
were anti-militarist or atheist anyway. Then he could attack
both General Staff and Church. Yet not if he respected
them.\* In such case he would praise their ability to change
their opinion. Every established body should be regarded as
equipped with individual soul and as fallible as any other
body, any other soul, capable of stumbling and of repenting.

\*       \*       \*

\* *When the* Salon des Artistes français *rejects Manet, Cézanne, Renoir,
but subsequently accepts them, it is the same jury's eyes opening.*

At the play I was astounded that Claudel's scenes jeered at one Church and praised another without shocking our judges, who were so severe about my cardinal and his manoeuvres—whereas they would never have allowed generals to turn somersaults.

The stupidity of the *Mariés de la Tour Eiffel* provoked a scandal and prevented a new run. That was a stupidity of vaudeville, neither more or less.

One is therefore obliged to recognise that some works exasperate, emitting strange distorting waves, provocative of injustice and there is nothing their authors can do about it save to understand that their protection is in invisibility but as good behaviour exacts withdrawal from their perspectives and contours.*

*      *      *

My play complete, I first put it in the hands of Jean Vilar. As my fixtures did not fit his, I then took it to Jean Louis Barrault. In a month I had the *mise en scène*, setting and costumes ready. The members of the Marigny Company, overburdened through alternating plays, got the idea into their heads that my script would be easy to learn. They soon found that the *Peter-Piper-picked-a-peck* style which I use to avoid slickness forced them to honour every single syllable. Otherwise, the texture gives way. They then got a taste for such grammatical acrobatics. Jean Louis Barrault himself proved a most impressive cardinal. He sounded like a prelate out of the Charterhouse of Parma. He looked like Raphaël's young cardinal.

We played, first to an audience of shopkeepers whose reaction was very favourable, secondly, to a special invited audience whose reactions one had to guess at, thirdly, to the general public and the judges. We achieved a block triumph. A block in which, leaving it in the cloakroom, people lost

* *Why is* Tête d'Or *never given again, seeing that this work's invisibility protects it?*

their individuality and were lost in that collective hypnosis
that our judges hate. They themselves became individuals
backwards, oyster-like just to be contrary. On the *gala* night,
François Mauriac, prompted by some blinding deaf-making
force, thought he heard and thought he saw a work which
was not mine, was outraged by it, and, when together with the
cast I was called to the footlights, demonstratively left the
theatre. A Sunday followed during which the company
interpreted *L'Echange*. I was in the country, resting. I had
guessed that Mauriac was going to write an article and was
rather amused at the idea of replying.

The following day, the article appeared. An "open letter".
A very poltroonly piece of flourish, from which oozed
complete misunderstanding of the world in which I live.
The trial of a fable which just does not concern me at all.

Even if he dislikes doing so, a man attacked at the Champs-
Elysées roundabout must defend himself. I added a few
little touches to the reply I had already drafted and published
it in *France-Soir* under the heading "My dear fellow, I accuse
you!" I could not reproach Mauriac with his bits of atavism
or his Bordeaux origins. I reproached him merely with an
error of judgement, with usurping the prerogatives of a
priest and with sitting himself down at the right-hand of
the Almighty.

Montaigne says: "What you are adducing is a local bye-
law, you just don't know what the universal law is.

"God is not your opposite number, your fellow-citizen,
your buddy, and if he has revealed himself in any way at all
to you, he did not do so to debase himself to your diminutive
stature, nor to put you in control of his might."

As a matter of fact, Mauriac has remained one of those
children who will insist on mixing with grown-ups. You can
see the breed in any hotel. Useless to say: "It's late, up you
go, off to bed." They refuse to obey and disturb everybody.
Mauriac himself once said to me: "I am an elderly child
disguised as Academician." But then, the fact that he is not

one of the family of intellects which he would like to have belonged to is always prompting him to write articles about those who are. The result of that is that even where at loggerheads among themselves those who really are members of the family band together against him, all because of his never-ending attempts to play a part in their internal squabbles and set one against another.

\*        \*        \*

François Mauriac gets home from the theatre. He sits himself down squarely at his table. He is about to write his *Prière sur l'Acropole*. Strange prayer, strange Acropolis. Strange reading for Carmelites. (He tells us that his open letter is on the reading list there). I would rather say that what he does is swing round, cast a glance at the human hunt trailing at my tail, then bravely puts his hunting horn to his lips to sound another little tally-ho.

Nothing is graver than to miss one's beast, it becomes dangerous. Mauriac does miss. But the animal is not spiteful. He happens to know his marksman. That, after all is said and done, is all I reproach him with.

\*        \*        \*

My reply was deliberately anti-literary. I was not shooting for the delection of the goddess of snipery. The sugariness of that Mauriac open letter displeased me more than any gall. It suggests to my mind my childhood plays and the sets which adorned them. I was depicted as chaining my old mother to a pillar at the *Marigny* (and insulting her). I was a satellite. I was in harlequin garb, carried by angels. Now, Mauriac is not naive, he knows quite well that my work had nothing in common with that of Appollinaire or Max Jacob (save the respect due both of them) and that my play is an objective examination of the roads leading to the Reformation, but it suited him to spike the wheels of the vehicle, and try to upset it. He lowered himself to a work of sabotage.

I imagine Mauriac rather expected his hunting-horn solo, his harlequinade, would rally the hunt at his heels. He was quite off the mark. Not only did the priesthood not follow him (as I had had proof in Germany), but he got a tin can tied to his own tail.

The clatter of that decorative thing lasted some time, in the form of letters and articles congratulating me and indeed rather importuning me, since I am still convinced that in all this Mauriac was very little responsible, for he was merely the instrument of those forces which are the subject of my study, a revolt of the forces of darkness struggling against the brilliant illumination of footlights and spotlights.

It will be thrown back in my face that the success of the play invalidates this theory. To that I shall reply that the curtailment of the show by the departure of the company on tour but confirms the theory. It was certainly one of the reasons why I applied to the *Marigny Theatre* in preference to others which had been asking me for *Bacchus* and which could have played it without the rhythm of alternate shows and without interruption breaking off at all.

Shall I add here that no doubt I took my play away from Vilar because the press was idolising him to spite Jean Louis Barrault whom it had idolised the day before, but suddenly de-idolised overnight, without any other reason than that fidgetiness of a metropolis which flits from idol to idol and finds pleasure only in breaking its own toys.

It is probable that against all logic and in secret obedience to orders more subtle than the demands of the visible world, it was this transfer of powers and the limited number of performances that made me make up my mind as I did.

\*     \*     \*

A stage play is more convincing than a film because a film is a tale of phantoms. The audience does not exchange waves with flesh and blood creatures. The film's strength is to placard what one thinks, proving it by a subjectivism which becomes objective, by irrefutable acts which are irrefutable because they take place before our eyes.

Thanks to the plainness of the vehicle, one succeeds in making the unreal realistic. Solely this realism wins against unreality, masking its cyphers and leaving the spectator outside.

A woman correspondent reproaches me with my films. In her view, in them I disclose to too many people what should remain concealed. Let me explain to her that the film undertakes to muddle up its secrets in no time and delivers them but to rare individuals, mingled in the crowd, which is distracted by the constant crush of new sights. All religions, I say again, and poetry is one, protect their secrets in the form of fables and let them be revealed only to those who would never know them if the fables did not disseminate them.

In the theatre the audience, elbow to elbow, produce a wave which wells and laps against the stage, to return enriched, at least if the actors are stirred by the feelings they simulate and not content merely to ape them, for that prevents the flow back.

My *Bacchus* company, worked up by stupid criticisms, gave their all to persuade. They succeeded.

It remains no less certain that it would be madness if one success after another blinded us. We should be no more impressed by the miscomprehensions resulting from success than those which win us sarcasm. For that would be to fall back into the pride of responsibilities. We should lose that lofty tree-like indifference, an indifference from which I reproach myself with being brought down but too often.

*          *          *

The soul is ridiculously feeble. Its principal weakness is to think itself powerful, to get convinced of this, when every experience is proof that it is never responsible for the forces it throws out and which turn against it the moment they put their noses outside.

*Note of October* 19*th,* 1932. *Bacchus* at the Düsseldorf *Schauspielhaus,* with Gründgens marvellous as the cardinal. In the midst of the interminable applause of an audience of equally stern catholicism or protestantism, and the following day, reading the remarkable studies of the newspapers, I did indeed ask myself whether the French and Belgian press alike had not been the victims of a phenomenon of collective hallucination.

*Note No.* 2. In an hotel, a priest, taking the death-rattle of a man in the next room for love-throes, hammered on the wall instead of going to the man's aid, that is what I think of, reading Mauriac's articles against Genet.

What frivolity under all those uniforms and honours! Frivolity charging others with it and banking only on the visible.

# On Permanent Waves

WHEN I was supervising the dyeing of my actresses' heads for the film *Orpheus*, I found it most interesting to keep my ears open and listen to the ladies' talk. Their helmets deafened them, so they spoke rather louder than they realised.

We are in a world in which the problems of the visible and invisible, of responsibility and irresponsibility, do not arise. A world faithful to the figure 4. A world which reminds one of little girl's description: "Cows are big animals with four feet which go right down to the ground."

Thus sit our ladies, very sure of being present. The Pharaonic helmets with which their hairdressers have coiffed them lend an air of regal might, their permanent waves adding permanence, turning them into Delphic sybils. The heat is on. They steam. They smoke. And from their tongues slip oracular pronouncements.

One indicates to her manicurist a young girl reflected in a series of mirrors. "Poor pet, her mother gives her an allowance of a million francs a month, how ever do you think she can manage on that?"

One helmeted Minerva unbosoms herself to another: "I tell you, I am only sensitive to little things. Big ones I can bear with fortitude. You know how little my son's death upset me. But I could never bear to be without my butter. Isn't it queer? That's my nature."

Pointing to an employee who was ill, a woman patient cried: "But just look at her. She's like death! Like death!" The sick employee heard this, and was most upset.

74

I could easily pile on further examples of infantile egotism. I thought of the gala shows to which these permanent waves would be invited, and I turned back to my modest interpreters, ranging from dark to blond as the experts decreed. I imagined the film, a veritable tunnel of mirrors into which I was to plunge and the hall imposed on us by the producers, where, proud of their spouses' curls, these ladies and their husbands would take their seats.

\*     \*     \*

During the German occupation, our ladies got their waves by the intermediary of poor devils who pedalled away in the basement, by leg-power ensuring the necessary volts.

Here the shade labours valiantly, alien to the body she perfects. A hand in a bowl of warm water, eyes on their own faces, all attention to the transmogrification, from the toils of which they expect a transfiguration, incapable of getting inside themselves, however could these ladies drop several floors below, and pity the invisible band drying their heads? Yet the juices which feed their rudimentary machinery are certainly the same as those which feed the complex machinery of genius. They have got a soul. Or rather, they have got *some soul*. Thanks to that soul (portion of soul) a vehicle functions in which invisible and visible are alike. The patience of such vehicles is unlimited in anything concerning the hope of external progress. As far as internal progress goes, self-satisfaction relieves them of all concern about it.

For, were a miracle to take place, were the basement pedallers to make any moral light, any fear, any uneasiness, any remorse, for home use, the débâcle would reveal what helmeted vacancy these minervas are. Absolute horror would make their "hair stand on end at the soup", as I heard one of them say. They would die sitting, their mouths open, as if crying out.

\*     \*     \*

There you have the audience to which we are condemned by an old indolence which will insist on taking them to be an élite. Money has changed hands and the élite has shifted its milieu. It has become legion. It crowds into theatre galleries where embracing couples watch and listen instead of watching each other. It is prone to emerge from itself, emitting waves which enrich the show. It collaborates. Whatever one offers it, it is not offended. It is merely offended with any place with prices which exclude it.

We can never congratulate Jean Vilar sufficiently on his enterprise. An enterprise to which, historically, I attach the greatest importance. In the theatres where they play *le Cid* and *le Prince de Hombourg*, one can rediscover what one had feared to lose. I also found it in Germany, where audiences arrive punctually, do not leave before the end, and applaud the actors.

For the permanent waves and their husbands arrive in the middle of Act I, and before the play is over scurry off to foregather with their ilk in bars where they criticise what they have just failed to see.

In all probability in those cyclists the fatigue of pedalling stationary bikes excited dreams far more like ours than the vague musings prompted by helmet fatigue.

*  *  *

Girls who work in those hells the agonies of which our ladies undergo heroically, tell us that the tortures lead to confidences. They stimulate psychoanalytic catharsis. Yet the things which then escape from the invisible serve but to illustrate those which one sees. The pot boils over. The girl who hears it is of the breed of the unknown cyclists. Anonymous. Merely a left-luggage office.

Thus the wavers void themselves of their void and that rounds off the seance. Double cure. They emerge completely renovated. As they slip off the white overall they imagine

that in the helmet and the hairdresser they have left behind
them both the colour which their hair was and the colour
which their souls were.

Mme. Chanel, a past-master of all this, arrived on the
Riviera after seeing Vilar's *Prince de Hombourg*. She relates
that just behind her were grounded two of these steam-
cooked dames, very apprehensive of all the young creatures
round them, thinking them all communists.

One of them examined the programme notes.

"This play's about a Boche," she whispered to her neighbour. "He is called Kleist and he has committed suicide."

"That's all to the good," said the other, "it's always one
less."

# On a Justification for Injustice

"Another accused man, Cocteau . . ."
Sartre: *Saint Genet.*

YOUTH is unjust. It owes it to itself so to be. It sets up
defences against the invasion of personalities stronger
than its own. For a time, it yields. Subsequently, it
assumes the defensive. Overnight, it begins to resist. The love
and confidence which dwelt within seem debility. Its
eagerness to combat this sickness finds it disarmed. It improvises weapons. It turns against the object of its confidence and tramples it underfoot, and does so the fiercer
since in so doing it also tramples on itself. It then imitates
the murderer who slashes away at the body already
inert.

It would be ungracious of me to complain of the icono-
clasm of youth. When I was young, did I not turn on my own
loves? And first and foremost on Stravinsky's *Sacre*, which
had so permeated my being that I took it for sickness and
tried to forearm myself against it. Youth, cursed to replace
fixation by fixation. One wonders (as Stravinsky did in the
sleeping car in the chapter *Birth of a Poem*) why I never
attacked the idolisation of Picasso. What Stravinsky meant
was: "Since it was a defensive reflex of youth in you to strike
out, why did Picasso, who also occupied every inch of your
territory, why did he not set off that reflex?" That no doubt
comes from the fact that Picasso is so quick with his matador
twists, his red cape flaring right just when one thinks it left
and the banderillas suddenly pricking our own necks. I loved
his cruelty, the way he decried what he loved. Never did a
man care more for his bees, don more veils, tin more to keep

78

his swarm on the move. All that distracts the enemy which
lurks in the heart of enamoured love.

*          *          *

Maurice Sachs had enormous charm. One can see it even
more since his death. I could not say where or how I first
met hini. Then he scarcely ever left my house. He haunted
the clinics in which my health compelled me to spend long
periods. His kindly face, so open, was so familiar to me that
the first memory of it is lost. If he pilfered me, it was merely
to buy me presents, and if I mention such petty thefts, that is
because they are to his honour.

When Maurice was without a penny, he stuffed his pockets
with so-called hygienic tissue. This he would rustle, fancying
his pocket stuffed with thousand-franc notes.

"It's just to give me confidence," he would say.

I ought not to complain of having been tricked. It hurt
only me. I have always preferred burglars to the police. Let
those who like it that way not be pinched from. Besides, a
man needs confidence. With Sachs, one had it. I repeat: he
gave more than he took and never took but to give. That sort
of purloining is not to be confused with common theft, let
alone with such as utilises a sort of inventive genius against
which no similar genius protects one.

*          *          *

One year, when I was staying at Villefranche, Maurice
loaded on to a barrow and carted off everything my Paris
chambers held: books, drawings, correspondence, manuscripts. He sold it all in bundles, without even checking it.
He imitated my signature marvellously. It was when I still
had a flat in Anjou Street. He had presented my mother
with a forged letter in which I gave him a free hand.

When he was managing a series for Gallimard's, round the
auction rooms went copies of Apollinaire and Proust, on
the fly-leaf of which he wrote these letters, He exhibited

them in the windows. As I was made responsible for that scandal, I put Gallimard wise. He summoned Sachs and told him he could not keep him on. Sachs asked for a few minutes. Off he went, to come back with a freshly-written letter from me, in which I begged him urgently to turn my books, correspondence and manuscripts into cash.

"You see," says Maurice, "how completely I forgive Jean his fantasies, I propose to burn this letter of authorisation."

He lit his pocket-lighter and did as he suggested. When Gaston Gallimard told me all about that fine trick, he said that his mind was only set at rest by that burning of the letter. We both had a jolly good laugh at Maurice's skill in proving himself innocent by making a forgery and burning it.

Even when unmasked, Maurice continued to diddle his dupes. His basic principle was that people were amused by the mishaps of others, and never for a moment feared that the same might happen to them. During the occupation, the Jews confided their furs and jewellery to him. And if I am asked what my attitude was on the Riviera when the book-shops informed me that they had a lot of dubious articles in their stock, I shall reply that I just couldn't care less. I would say I "had the *cagne*", which is a speciality of Toulon, best illustrated if I say that there was a time when if the Chief of Police came on a man with that particular devil in him lying sound asleep in the roadway, he carefully drove round him and went his way. Southern French *la cagne* is the *dolce far niente* of the Italians, and Maurice was a great *cagnard*. His *agne* was really fattening, too, he used to wallow in it.

\*          \*          \*

One morning, after a year of silence, he suddenly rang me up, a little before his departure for Germany. He was about to die, he said, at the *Hôtel de Castille* and begged me to go there. And in a room of that hotel I did find him, in bed, very pale.

"You are the only man I have ever loved. Your friendship stifled me and I tried to get away from it. I wrote lies and outrageous things about you and against you. Forgive me. Orders for their destruction have been issued."

Maurice did not die at the *Hôtel de Castille*. He met his end at Hamburg, in lamentable circumstances. His books were not destroyed. On the contrary, they continue to appear, some owing to the intervention of a friend we had in common, Yvon Bélaval. Others are waiting. Those are in the possession of Gérard Mille.

\*          \*          \*

I do not agree with my friends that these insults anger. Maurice told me the truth, his truth, for we all have our own truths. I hold that the insulting things about me are evidence of a profound impression. At least, that is the angle I see them from. As I have revealed at the beginning of this chapter, he forged whatever weapons he wanted and attacked me all ways. One guesses that he did not really believe any of the things he said. And any person unable to understand why he attacked me and himself as he did cannot possibly understand his writings. He drew his vital juices from that wild urge to get rid of whatever distended him. His method at once offensive and defensive and his path to the death which one might take to be flight was its consecration.

\*          \*          \*

Maurice Sachs is a perfect example of self-defence against an invader. The more he wounded, the more he lashed out at himself. For he did also beat his own breast just as his co-religionists do at the Wailing Wall in Jerusalem. It was by thus intoxicating himself by blows that he fascinated and knew posthumous success. But his cynicism interested nobody unless it was all confessions and lies. He interests us because he lived on a passionate plane. Maurice passionately loved both his fellow-men and himself. His works are the battle-ground of the war between those two feelings which he waged. His youth prevented him making them live together. If he was to live, he had to kill. But beyond the visible man he did not see. The other escapes him.

The roads which led him to that method were long. He gave himself to friendship frankly and without *arrière-pensée*. Neither Max Jacob nor I had anything to complain of his friendship. He respected us. He never got on intimate terms in speech with me. I certainly addressed him as *thou*. Generally speaking, the younger generation are insensitive to the shade of distinction in French when one passes from *you* to *thou*. I have often been troubled to hear very young poets addressing Max Jacobs in the singular.

\*          \*          \*

After *le Potomak*, I was determined to construct an ethic for myself. But it was far from being ready when I went over to the attack. Maurice had no ethic at all. Then, most cleverly, he resolved to have a negative one for himself, a sort of de-ethicised ethic. From that moment he lent all his active idleness to it. None of us suspected that all the time his pen was busy. One never saw him write. True, he began writing when the attitude of my friends had already made me cease to have anything to do with him.

He wrote without ceasing. He narrated himself. He had the courage to emphasise himself by exhibiting what people call depravities, though they were merely subservience to instincts condemned by the morals of the moment. As for the confessions about his sexuality, in her machine Nature always makes mincemeat of social proprieties. The films of the vegetable kingdom of which I have spoken above are an indication of that. It is by risky use of sex that Nature switches from parsimoniousness to prodigality. For if these creatures only used the pleasure which accompanies the reproductive act for that sole purpose, Nature would overload her dwelling. She prompts to visible disorder in order to

protect her invisible order. Such sensible disorder was once to
be observed in the South Sea Islands. The young natives submitted to standards reluctantly and the women gave birth in
cow-dung, so that none but tough children should survive.
Until the Europeans went there to introduce order, that is to
say to bring in clothing, alcohol, sermons, excess population
and death.

Sachs did not look so far. He slid down his own slope. That
slope will perhaps deliver an instructive case to that court
whose sentence is feared by young folk who feel guilty. I know
that he boasts brassily and cheats. But, taking all in all,
reading between the lines, I approve his running counter to
the hypocrites. I also approve his wild efforts to plead a
forgery so one might guess at the truth.

*          *          *

If I try to recall Maurice, it is not in his books that I
discover him. It is in those passionate years in which the
politics of letters split our côteries, grouping them and
setting one at loggerheads against another. Maurice trotted
from one camp to the other. He did not betray. He listened,
laughed, helped, went on all fours if he could but be useful.
I often scolded him.

When he entered the seminary, I warned Maritain. I knew
he had gone in there to run away from his debts. Maritain
took no notice of me. His nobility had faith in the refuge. It
would save Maurice from more serious debts and the return
would be generous. Thus Maurice became a seminarist. We
saw him, cassock-garbed, introducing American cigarettes
and a hip-bath into his cell. His charming grandmother,
Mme. Strauss, had been made most anxious because by the
lack of ablutory facilities there.

One day, at Juan-les-Pins, as Maurice had begun to behave
very badly, I advised him to resume lay attire. He was
already getting bored with the part he was playing. He submitted goodnaturedly, and such was his charm that the

G

Revd Father Pressoir, the Provincial of the Seminary, reproached me with having been "very smart at my job."

Poor Maurice. Had he not been one of the vanguard of a period in which commandos of all sorts were in fashion, what would the world have known of him? I approve of his having lent his frailties an air of strength. Right or wrong, my ethic requires me to forgive his and to accept it in my Pantheon.

*       *       *

Claude Mauriac will furnish me my second example.

His father was the friend of my youth. Hence I adopted him like a son. I was then living in Madeleine Square. My house was open to him. If it pleases you to have the entrée of my house, have it, by all means! If you like it there, stay! I abjure foresight. And were I asked what I should carry from my house were it to burn, my reply would be: *fire!*

At Versailles, where I was beginning *la Machine à Écrire*, and where he had accompanied me, he asked me if I should be disturbed if he jotted down some of my pronouncements. It was his regret that people knew me poorly, he had in mind a book on me. I was able to prevent the note-taking, which I disliked. I could not prevent the book. He offered it with the best of intentions.

You know the book, of course. Friendship all a-sparkle with insults and inaccuracies. Claude produces lies, but his great gambit is to charge me with them. He was to tell a journalist that he was very fond indeed of me, it stood out a mile. In due course he proved it. We happened to meet in Venice, in the *Piazza San Marco*, after a private showing of *Parents Terribles*. I was the more ready to forgive him since I have a loathing for feuds and I knew what motivated him. I had taken the machinery of it to pieces in the case of Sachs.

In two remarkable articles, Claude praised *Orpheus*. But the reflex still worked. He could not bring himself to be guided by his heart. He published a new article in which he withdrew his opinion, making out that *Orpheus* had dropped in price and had a cool reception. It would have been under-standable for him to attack the audience. He attacked the film. But the patience of my ethic is unlimited, and I should rather like the winding road eventually to bring Claude to make himself one. Sachs's would hardly do.

I have an idea that he came to regret his last article. A recent letter from him suggests so much. The *Bacchus* business saved us from resort to buckets of cold water.

\*          \*          \*

The attitudes of Maurice and Claude are not similar and are not related. Maurice babbled. Claude ruminates. But in them both we see the mark of youth closed to enthusiasms. This anxiety about enthusiasm is as frequent in the younger generation as "the anxiety of the act" observed by psycho-analysts. There is even a sort of counter-enthusiasm gaining ground. It draws its vital force from the fear of letting oneself go and being found doing so, shyness here transmuting into invective. Kindness becomes synonymous with stupidity, spitefulness synonymous with intelligence. As Hans puts it to the cardinal in *Bacchus*: *Le drame est là*; that *is* the play.

\*          \*          \*

Age brings us a sturdy health which is no longer worried about invasions. If alien forces do enter our territory, we know how to withdraw, how to provide them with scorched earth where without contaminating our own forces they come to grief. We no longer fear admiring contradictory works of art, we no longer want to rise above them. They become our guests and we offer them a regal reception.

\*          \*          \*

Gide obeyed the mechanism of youth. He was entangled in it to the very end. I should not mention him in this chapter were it not that he throws light on its purpose by his use of procedures which are unconscious in the young, though quite conscious in him. His longing for youth would get him mixed up in schemes in which he forgot his age. He then behaved with a frivolity which in the end he had to try to explain away. So he will furnish me with a sort of marginal third example, the more striking since here the defences are understood, the weapons crooked.

In this chapter, in which I am trying to make excuses for my assailants, I have to extend the framework to find excuses for Gide attacking me in his paper, and to elucidate the part played by the young vehicles which ran to and fro between us.

*     *     *

It was in 1916, I had just published le Coq et l'Arlequin and Gide was offended. He was apprehensive lest the younger folk should be diverted from his programme, and also afraid of losing votes. He summoned me like a schoolmaster a pupil and read out an open letter addressed to me.

Now, I get quite a lot of open letters. In this one of Gide's, I was apparently a squirrel, Gide a bear at the foot of the tree, with me hopping about from branch to branch. In short, a dressing-down, which I was to receive in public. I told him forthwith that I should have to reply to that open letter. With a snort, in a hoity-toity manner he said very well, if that's how you want it, nothing richer or more instructive than such exchanges.

No doubt it is realised that Jacques Rivière refused to publish my reply in the Nouvelle Revue Française where Gide's letter appeared. I will admit, it was a bit blunt. In it I made the observation that the villa Montmorency where Gide lived did not face square to the street, its windows were all on one side.

Gide had already been given one such bucket of cold water, which was from Arthur Cravan from whom he pinched Lafcadio. Cravan was an easy-going giant. He came to see me, and sprawled full length, showing himself off, feet above

head. He confided to me the pages in which ᴜ˟    ˙ of a visit
Gide made to his attic, a visit very like that of Julius de
Varaglioul.

But from those pages and that visit Gide in his usual way
made good profit. But there was no making any profit out of
my reply. All he could do with that was try to answer it, and
he did not fail to have a shot. Gide adored notes big and
little, and replies to replies. He answered mine in *Ecrits
Nouveaux*, which had published it.

Shall I confess it, I never even read the thing? I felt I
simply must protect myself from mere reflex action, also
against opening the sluice gates of open letters. Time passed.
Montparnasse and cubism came along, Gide keeping out of
the way. He was a past-master at forgetting insults, especially
those which came from his own pen. He suddenly rang me
up and asked me if I would be uncle to, well, let's call him
Olivier. He said this disciple of his, Olivier, was *getting bored
with his library*. Well, I introduced young Olivier to the
cubists, to the work of young composers, and to the circus,
in which we adored the huge orchestra, the acrobats and
the clowns.

I did my stuff, but with a bit of caution. I knew my Gide
and his almost feminine jealousy. Now, young Olivier found
it very funny to tease Gide, singing my praises till poor Gide
had to clap his hands to his ears. He assured Gide he scarcely
ever left my side and had learned *le Potomak* by heart. This I
was not to learn about till 1942, before I went to Egypt. Gide
then unbosomed himself and assured me that he had wanted
to murder me (yes, his very words!) It was from this story
that the half-nelsons of his diary arose. At least, they have
been put down to it.

But what Gide did not confess was that I had had a
terribly difficult task over persuading him to read Proust.
Proust he considered a society author. No doubt he was
annoyed with me for having succeeded in convincing him,
when suddenly Proust filled the *Nouvelle Revue Française* with

his marvellous scrawl. The review's office was full of it. There were several tables busy deciphering.

At Gallimard's publishing office, on the day Proust died, Gide whispered to me: "Now I shall only have a bust here."

\*　　　\*　　　\*

In himself he combined Rousseau the botanist and Mme. d'Épinay's Grimm. He suggested to me an interminable and heart-rending day coursing after hapless hares. He combined the terror of the hare and the cunning of the hounds. One could find confounded in him both hunt and hunted.

Rousseau's posterior was Freud's moon rising. Gide had a loathing for such exhibitionism. But if one countered him, one found Voltaire's smile.\*

\*　　　\*　　　\*

I shall not linger over those responsible for those distortions of the truth which twist my most trivial gestures out of shape. I have made my own attitude clear elsewhere. Speaking of Gide, my only thought was of the labyrinth into which he used to draw young people, loving to lose himself with them in it. The machinery of rebellion started into action after his death. His dead body was abused. That is his safeguard. He had been too much exploited, commented on, scratched over, exhausted. His invisibility was merely visibility under examination. He will profit by the iconoclasts. He will get a little rest there. He used to confess little things to hide the big ones. The big ones will come to the surface and save him.

\*　　　\*　　　\*

I was fond of Gide and he exasperated me. I exasperated him and he liked me. We were quits. I recall that when he was writing his *Oedipus* after my *Oedipuses* (*Oedipus the King*,

* *When I asked Genet why he refused to meet Gide, he replied: "You have to be either defendant or judge. I can't abide judges who slobber over their defendants."*

*Antigone, Oedipus Rex, la Machine Infernale*) he informed me of this in the words: *"there is a regular Oedipemic."* He was a past master at pronouncing the syllables of difficult words. He seemed to fish them up out of a water-butt.

At the summit of his life he came to my country house with Herbart. He would have liked me to produce a film version of *Isabella* which he was making. From the look in Herbart's eye I could see that he was stuck with it. It was a mediocre film. I explained this to him in a written note, and said that from him one rather expected something like the *Faux-Monnayeurs* or the *Caves*. He was jubilant, hearing me read a note. He stuffed it into his pocket. It is possible it will be found in a drawer somewhere.

Our meetings were pleasant to the end—to the letter in which Jean Paulhan described him to me as petrified on his deathbed.

*    *    *

None the less, it is surely clear enough that there are people who know how to hurt others and those whose task it is to swallow the insults. I shall be reproached with attacking my assailants. I am not attacking them. I am only pondering their responsibilities and irresponsibilities. Visible and invisible together. Gide, Claude Mauriac, Maurice Sachs, really put off the day when they bone me and eat all my marrow. Without realising it, they do me a service.

For that matter, I hold that the effluvia which provoke a certain sort of attack come much more from the defendant than the judge. In a zone in which there is no going to law to determine who is responsible, judge and defendant are both of them equally responsible and irresponsible.

# On Relative Liberties

"I AM quite prepared to show my pictures, but not myself." This is what I told the Paris journalist who was advising me to arrange an exhibition of my canvases in Paris.

For once, I have the right at once to serve invisibility and myself. A rare enough happening for me to want to profit by it.

I had had the opportunity of seeing my canvases and tapestries hung (not hanged) in the rooms of Munich's new *Pinacotheca*, or *Haus der Kunst*. There was a studious sort of crowd of viewers. I know what the word would be in Paris: "What next won't the fellow meddle in? Why does he paint? Who authorised him?" And other little courtesies which I will leave out.

I am no painter and do not flatter myself that I am one. I painted to have a rest from drawing, drawing being a sort of writing, and ordinary calligraphic activity happening to have bored me. I painted to make a new vehicle for myself. I painted because I liked doing it. Painting eliminates intermediaries. I painted, just think of it, because it was my pleasure to paint.

It is always on the boards that I may give it up and that this vehicle may disturb my all-powerful tenebrosity, this being embarrassed by having to appear in broad daylight, revealing itself in broad daylight with a coat of paint for features.

These canvases and tapestries will live as suits them. They will suffer and move about like people free to go where they list. While I write these lines, they are on the way from

Munich to Hamburg, thence to go on to Berlin, and in those towns other galleries and other eyes will see them.

Two gay summers (that of 1950 and that of 1951), two summers in which I tattooed the villa Santo Sospiro like so much skin, then began handling all the paraphernalia of the painter. Two summers in which I became wall and canvas, obedient to my own instructions, without any court to judge me.

Between you and me, fair game. They may destroy my canvases and me too. But the perspective of time and space rules out the destruction of the invisibility of it. For a work of art overflows its own being. Even destroyed, it forges on. Knossos flavours its ruin with it.* What have we left of Heraclitus? Yet he speaks to us, is our friend.

*             *             *

If I write, I upset people. If I shoot a film, I upset them. If I paint, I upset them. If I exhibit my painting, I upset them and I equally upset them if I don't show. A genuine gift for upsetting. I reconcile myself to it, for I should like to win through. But even when I am dead I shall upset people. My work will have to bide till another slow death is accomplished—that of this gift for upsetting. Even so, it may emerge victorious, no longer then embarrassed by myself, but crying out in its youngness: Phew!

That has been the fate of many an enterprise which I respect, a fate which our age, convinced as it is of being omniscient, ultra-lucid, nothing escaping its eye, thinks unlikely. It is deceived, invisibility making use of countless tricks, prestidigitorial, never repetitive.

*             *             *

* Little by little at Knossos those domed hives, the low hills of Crete, lead us to the open hive of the palace, this nothing less than the labyrinth that Daedalus built for Minos. The portraits which the frescoes contain offer wasp-waisted damsels flitting bee-like flower to flower, busy perhaps making the golden honey of which is made the frieze in the Candia museum (with its two bees face to face).

How can one paint without being a painter, I mean—a born painter? One of those who escape analysis? Type. Auguste Renoir, a knotty tree blooming all the year round. Night come, Renoir would clean his brushes on little canvases which became masterpieces—I am the owner of a number of them. The remark was made to Renoir: "You ought to be proud of your works fetching such prices in the sale rooms." And Renoir's reply: "You don't ask a horse if it is proud of winning the Grand Prix, do you?"

It remains to stick up a few teasers and try to solve them. To get a notion of a feasible picture, copy the idea till your picture resembles it. Organise a meeting between the abstract and the concrete. Failing science (or prescience) extract light from yourself and hand the result round, for better or worse. Our tenebrosity does not hate new machinery. It is less tyrannical. How quiet it is! From such calm, something comes into being. Good or bad, the canvas I looked squarely at looks squarely out at me, till I no longer dare look at it, staring back at me as it does. Though, for that matter, it too does get tired of it. But it takes on a disturbing life which detaches itself from our own and then makes mock of us. It is of little concern what it depicts. It has sucked profound forces from us. It draws from them a youthfulness which our years beat back. Scornful of our years, it bids them be circumspect. Itself, it is not. And I am proud of feeling free to show or not show my canvases. They are free to disobey me.

\*     \*     \*

What a queer book this is! Most defiant. It repeats itself. It pushes me about all ways. Tail-biting, it marks a circle in which the same syllables are constantly writ. How heavy the terms *visibility*, *invisibility* do weigh! How I should like to spare the reader such a burden. But what can I do about it? They are dictated to me. And if I rise in revolt, I am inspired by what is dictated to me. I congratulate myself on being in flight, then I find myself back where I started from.

I am constantly finding myself in the state in which might be a two dimensional creature dwelling in a two dimensional house and unable to conceive of a curve. It steps on to a globe, trudges away, escaping, getting farther off, then one day sees before it the house from which it fled and which it left behind it.

*Le Potomak, la Fin du Potomak, Opium, Essai de Critique indirecte*, such a lot of books in which I idled round and round a void. This time I am tackling that void, inspecting it, trying to detect it in the act of betrayal. *Just try, just try*! whispers a fatal hide-and-seek. Just as when people "hide" something right under our noses and laugh at our blundering failure to find it. But I keep on. For it does sometimes happen that one tricks the tricksters. It is, so it seems to me, the poet's job to track down the stranger and, if the stranger decoys him as he does *Orpheus*, by the horse of my play or the Rolls Royce of my film, *Orpheus* is not thereby less concerned in his reign. He dares the invisible. He gambles for the loser to win, whereas those who serve the visible gamble for the winner to lose.

\* \* \*

And all that: pictures, drawings, poems, plays, films, are of the time and space which is partitioned up, a great folded density of time and space. That density resists partition. All one sees are dents, rents, gaps, alien one to the other. On the inside of the fold, those gaps, rents, dents form lace, geometrical patterns. Time and space would have to unfold for us to be able to see them. That is why I admire Picasso's passion for chopping that density up, unfolding that which is non-unfoldable. Hatred of surfaces. Hatred driving him to smash everything, making of it something other, then smashing that something other because he is infuriated, smashing it to make files of it, to saw, fret away at the bars of his prison till he can twist them open.

What glimmering can those who believe art to be a luxury

have of our rebellions? Do they know that we are slaughter-houses? Do they know that our works are convicts escaped from the galleys? Do they know that this is why we are fired upon and harried by hounds?

I too get furious, with my ink, my pen, my miserable vocabulary, within which I fidget like a squirrel thinking it is a courser.

# On Translations

IN the train. *First passenger*: What is the time? *Second passenger*: Tuesday. *Third passenger*: Then this must be my station.

It is hard to comprehend one another.

In a Padua hotel, a tourist asks the porter if he can direct him to the Giottos. *Reply*: Down the corridor, on the right.

It is hard to comprehend one another.

Were the earth farther from the sun, it would still not be able to know if it is cooling, and to the sun, indeed, it would look like a sun. They would warm themselves mutually without heat.

It is hard to comprehend one another.

It is difficult above all to comprehend one another on this earth where the various languages rear impassable barriers between works of art. When such do get over the walls, it is by scrambling up one side and falling from the other in some disguise which fools the police. They are rare authors which have benefited by that operation.

It is not enough for translation to be marriage, it needs to be a love match. I am assured that Mallarmé, Proust, and Gide have been lucky in this. I nearly had my stroke of luck in Rilke. He had begun to translate *Orpheus*. But Rilke is dead.

Of my work, there are translations going the rounds so idiotic that one really wonders if the translator read me at all. What then is the origin of the praise which other countries heap on one? I imagine we have here a sort of vapour which while not reproducing the shape of the vessel, does suggest an active ghost of the contents. The djinn of an Arabian fable fit to move an auditorium.

The metamorphosis of a work of art changing its tongue

suggests ideas deriving from its original grace but no longer belonging to it. On our Riviera, under Mt. Agel, there is a cape now called Dog's Head. It was a Roman castrum. The *tête de camp*, or head of the camp, has in Nice dialect become —it is pronounced exactly the same—*Tête de Can*, which in that dialect is Dog's Head. And so today everybody perceives the dog's head in our cape! How do I know if our translated work does not thus assume profiles fitting legends about it? It may be just as an atmosphere can replace outlines, this being precisely the process of fame.*

At the Jacobi-Goethe House in Düsseldorf, where the Municipality dined me, the Mayor declared that Goethe was Germany's great unknown. "He is venerated, but people avoid reading him. He is so high up that all we see are his feet." I think that was well said. The prestige of a work attracts that respect which make it impossible for the Chinese ever to look at their Emperor. For if one did look, one was blinded. Far better start off blind.

\*         \*         \*

The true fame is after all when judgement ends, when visible and invisible are hashed together, and the public does not acclaim the show, but the idea it has derived from it, acclaiming itself for having had such *nous*. That sort of fame is the droit de seigneur of actors, for actors cannot wait. Their tenebrosity is not very dense and with all its strength leaps up into the light. The immediacy which they serve drives them to this. That is how it came about that we applauded Mme. Sara Bernhardt the moment she came on to the stage, she needed but to open her mouth, or be silent, make a gesture, walk out, compelling the stage to salute her more than to act, this acclaim being appraisal not at all of her speech or gestures, but of the fact that despite her age she could still attempt it. The audience was thus applauding

---

\* *See Naples and die, in French is*: voir Naples et mourir, *which should really be*: voir Naples et les Maures—*see Naples and the Moors!*

itself for having the perspicacity to understand that this actress was not making a gesture or speaking because the part required it, but was producing a *tour de force* to honour them. It was all admiration for itself that waves of fame should wash up at its feet a mythical monster, the stories of mother or grandmothers revealed in flesh and blood. The case is also cited of a famous Russian singer able to produce the highest note known. At a farewell concert he gave, all the celebrities of Petersburg, gathered to hear him, applauded so loudly when he merely opened his mouth to produce that note, that nobody really knows whether he did produce it or not.

*　　　*　　　*

Back now to our modest fame. The wanderings of translated works bear no relation to the pain it cost us to write them. That is justice. They are on the grand tour. They are sick of our detestable surveillance. That is why I take care not to complain. That is why I applaud the many German actresses who play *la Voix Humaine.* They serve texts so strange that they weep more than they make anyone else weep. Which is annoying and comes from the fact that the tear-making plant is out of order. Doubtless the march of the age in which we live is to blame. It would be risible to be too moved by it all. It was the thing for writers to be greatly moved in ages when they thought they inhabited a lasting and attentive world. As far as I go, I do not take it tragically. I was born with open hands. Writings and money slip from my fingers. Let those who wish to profit, do so. I am happy writing my works, because it is impossible for me to keep quiet and become a mortal secret.

For that matter, I find myself astonished that any contact with other people is feasible. For others only notice in us what fits their level. The girl who was prompter in *The Eagle has Two Heads* was always talking to me about Edwige Feuillére's pretty feet. That was what she saw pass to and fro in front of *her* nose.

When I attend a film sequence shot the day before, I turn oyster to the specialists. Everybody judges according to his speciality. The cameraman by the light, the chief operator by his rail, the script-girl by the position of the chairs, the actor according to his lines. I alone remain in real judgement.

\*     \*     \*

⌐Opinion is modelled on opinion. You have to have a start. As nobody dares take the initiative, they all eye each other. For that matter, a tendency to mistrust one's judgement should rather tend to egg the individual on to speak out against what he experiences. Prudence prevents him doing this and (except in a town like ours, where people get out of it by a hail of insults), prompts respectful hesitation. This hesitation gives the invisible time to fasten its bags and take flight before opinion makes up its mind and smothers the work under a layer of errors.

Then individual translations begin. Their orchestra creates cacophony. It is in the midst of this that the artist strives to extricate himself from the visible while the invisible buries its gold.⌐

\*     \*     \*

There must be a powerful impulse at the outset if at the end of its trajectory anything of a translated work is to remain and a foreign readership gets even a glimpse of us. *The Eagle has Two Heads* triumphed in London in an inaccurate adaption because of its leading lady. In New York it flopped in a still more inaccurate adaption, based on the English one, by the actress who played the part of the queen.

If by a miracle we obtained the gift of tongues, we should not recognise the books which charm us. And if there happen to be personal memories linked with the errors of such translated books and indeed confused with them, no doubt we should be sorry to lose them.

It can on occasion happen that in its native land a book

remains in the shadows, to come into the light in another. Which demonstrates how in a work of art the invisible can be more important than the visible.

Our collaboration in our writings seemed to suggest some sequel. We were flattering ourselves. The work soon does without us. We were merely its midwife.

\*       \*       \*

Leonardo da Vinci was lucky enough to say nearly everything in the international tongue of draughtsmanship. His writings are accompanied by explanatory sketches. His blackboard with its white chalk scribbles was often addressed to a class of boorish pupils. But the chalk remains, and finds its translation in exegesis. That is what is happening in the case of my 1930 film, *le Sang d'un Poète*. The exegetists are translating it in America. Through them I find myself understanding some of the things I put into it. Which by no means means that I did not put them there. On the contrary. For an invisible layer of the film (invisible to myself) belongs to the excavations of the archaeologists of the soul, who piece together the orders which directed my work without my suspecting its meaning. I realised this about it in the end when I was interrogated and found myself offering explanations copying those of others. At the outset I understood myself very little. I only saw the visible. That is being blinded by one's own creations.

The explanations are of all sorts. Some informed me that the film paraphrased the life of Christ, that the snow in which the schoolboy's footprint is made represents the veil of Veronica and that it was the fact that Fontenoy was the scene of the Eucharistic Congress that put into my lips the sentence: "While the cannon of Fontenoy thundered afar." This particular explanation came from a centre of study where the young pupils lent an obscene meaning to the factory chimney which at the beginning leans, to collapse at the end. As far as I had known the factory chimney was merely meant

H

to express that in this particular film there was no duration, that all the sequences took place while the chimney was falling. None the less, it is true that this explanation, like others, did worry me, just as any assertion can.

In my old film Freud made a rather rash early plunge. Some found the film icy, sexless, others—full of unhealthy sexiness. Now that was indeed a visual work *translated into several tongues*.

It is the fortune of upholstered works to be translated into several languages. If it does stunt our own perspicacity, the invisible has nothing against others digging into it. That complicates the maze in which it hides. Work which is too obvious attracts only tourists, who rush past it with a wild air and much consultation of their Baedekers.

Twenty years after the *Sang d'un Poète*, *Orpheus* was translated into every tongue. I mean of course the visual words. The writing of the words is kept down to sub-titles to which no serious person pays any attention. Germany taught me a lot about the mysteries of that film. Its quality of attention, research, its philosophical, metaphysical and metapsychical inheritance make it apt for excavations of this sort. A thousand German letters submit to me finds made in my soil for me to pronounce on. Some of them are still soiled with lava and oxides, and I pick out the gold because neither the oxides nor the lava can harm that.

Gradually the archaeologists offer me my film from an angle I never saw it from, and force me to pay attention to it. Here we have a phenomenon of exchanges which would be prevented if the work remained untranslated.

*     *     *

One has to avoid the music of a phrase and give it solely rhythm, leaving this the regularity of a beat. Prose must be derhymed, because rhymes soften the angles, or else rhymed deliberately, step by step. In French one has to keep things piling up by *quis* and *ques*, otherwise the language tends to

flow too smoothly. One has to erect dykes by bringing the
reader up against harsh consonants, by syncope of over-long
sentences, by over-short sentences. One must sense whether
a short or long syllable (masculine or feminine) should
precede this or that comma or full-stop. One should never
slip back into the garlanded stuff which people think is
style. . . . One should keep on and on re-writing (what might
be called the Penelope complex), which is what these efforts
to express myself become in a foreign tongue in which one
kids oneself that the ideas come over, for it would be unthinkable for the actual physical reality of one tongue to be
replaced by that of another or to suggest that they can
excite equal love.

*         *         *

It is to my advantage to know a language badly for translating purposes. I am more bothered by an article in a German
or English newspaper than by a poem by Shakespeare or
Goethe. A great text has its own contours. My antennae sense
this just as the blind read Braille. If I knew any of these
languages too well, a poem would discourage me by the unbridgeable obstacle of its equivalents. Knowing a language
badly, I caress the words, feel them, cup them, snuffle them,
turning them all ways. I sense the slightest rugosities of the
sound track. In the end my soul fingers those asperities like a
gramophone needle. The actual music embodied in the
groove does not thereby come out, but the Chinese shadow of
that music does. A Chinese shadow which fits the essence
well enough.

Let us beware of a translation of one of our texts if it seems
a true translation because it resembles it. That is the same as
a bad portrait. Better be openly misled.

A method the inverse of mine can be defended. One and
the other are equivalent or of equal value. There is often less
risk when one of our compatriots transports us to a foreign
tongue. Our French language is full of snares, words with

two spellings or two meanings. Nothing is harder for the
foreigner than to follow all their breaks and ellipses. In
addition, there is the use I make of commonplace words in
new lighting. Translated literally, my commonplace words
turn into gourmet's offerings. When *la Voix Humaine* appeared
in English dress I saw that the commonplace words *il rôde
comme une âme en peine* had assumed a Byronic lyricism.*

⌐The best thing at some distance is to let a work find its own
feet. Doing what it wants is just what it dreams of.⌐ If it is
happy, so much the better, for it scorns the care we continue
to take of it, indeed, is exasperated by it, like a son by the
nagging of a mother who can neither grasp that he has
grown up—or grown uglier.

---

* *A country Catholic in dark origin can speak* lightly *of "trapesing about
like a soul in purgatory" where an England with its protestant tenebrosity
speaks merely of a "cat on hot bricks".*—Translator.

# A Byway

THE invisible has its own paths, we ours. It does not
share our need to enlarge ourselves. If it can get out of
us, that suffices for it. To it there is little sense either in
our role of slave, or the fatuity which gives us the idea that
we are free. We serve merely to serve it. The praises earned
by its efforts are not really addressed to us. We usurp the
honours, that is all, rigging ourselves out with the titles and
heraldic devices which it lets us accept because they are
not of its realm at all. What is its realm? I do not know.
Every day brings me new proof that it is not mine, that I
should be making a fool of myself to rate myself so high. This
however does not prevent me going hot and cold at the insults
or words of praise which I harvest. To that I confess and in
some annoyance with myself. I am often ashamed of the
privileges which I usurp and after accepting reject, when
this I should have done in advance. But I am too weak to
have the pluck to do this when the offer is made. Next it is
too late. Thus my silence is partly responsible for all the fuss
of which I so disapprove. My only safeguard is that I do add
one more misunderstanding to those already there and thus
add to my disguise. Having an offer for an exhibition of my
paintings in Germany, I accepted, out of fear of showing them
in France, whereas I should really have shown them nowhere.
And just look, as I write these very lines, the illusion of
responsibility advises me to accept as my own errors which
are ascribed to me, and exaggerate my tendencies the wrong
way, letting myself think it is all my natural penchant.
For from all the errors and weaknesses which I imagine

subsequently to be set right by the daring which is also dictated to me are built up the constrasts germane to the creation of nature.

When we sieve the great, what we admire in them could not be without that for which we reprove them. To give birth to them, the invisible inflicts this caricature of their self on them, a mocking cartoon of personality. Thanks to such trickster's devices, the invisible gets a foothold and manages to scramble free, detracting men's eyes from itself by fixing them on the vehicular scapegoat whose horns are gay with medals and ribbons. For without the worst the invisible could never get a hold. That is the way it takes root, that is the way its stem grows away from us. It could never do so if it did not overwhelm us with what it avoids, without grafting on us success and scandal, by that magnetism which is usual in us and without which we should not be noticed. If it respected us, we should be pleonastic to it. a vehicle enjoying its prerogatives, a double, piling invisible on invisible without giving it room to grow.

Its own safeguard it finds in our becoming the hunted game in its stead—finely feathered too.

The moment it has once tricked us, it begins to consider its next one. While it waits, it prompts us into a thousand acts which serve it well but disserve us.

It knows quite well that though I see through it all, that doesn't matter in the least. Its next venture will find me just as stupid and disarmed as ever.

There you have the origin of the tortures of poets, tortures for which they know themselves responsible and of which they make every effort to believe themselves responsible, just to give themselves substance and bear with life to the end.

Many poets have not been able to bear the idea of this. Some by suicide, others by alcohol, yet others by some form of withdrawal or flight, have succeeded in avoiding their obligations, doing so all the easier if they happen to have already served their purpose, so that the invisible no longer

cares about their aid. Thus Rimbaud swept helpless through
Paris in a cab with his sister from the Northern to the
Southern Railway station at the very moment when Verlaine
in hospital was beginning his famous article, and would not
even set eyes on the city in which the invisible had already
exacted his whole being, and was now about to follow on his
heels all the way to Marseilles to harry him and punish his
rebellion.

I am still unable to tell how I shall get out of it. Whether
I shall have to break free from the invisible or this may want
to shake me off. These are matters too obscure for anyone to
venture into them. It is already dangerous to make rash
excursions into the darkness.

\*      \*      \*

Up to the age of twenty I thought that a poet could follow
his fantasy. What I got out of that was nonsense.\* At the end
a cold douche awaited me, and wasn't it cold too! For if the
invisible adopts us as vehicles, it compels us to go through
the whole training, which youth is least ready to admit.
Youth aims at the immediate and at success. After that cold
shower came many years of inclemency. Time alone can
teach us. The pride of youth prevents us from understanding
that servants' school, with a headmaster who only gives us
exeats to play the valet somewhere. Escapades. And corrects
such escapades with a lambasting.

\*      \*      \*

I observed that the ethic which I built up for myself in
order to make this unbearable régime bearable was beginning
to prove contagious for those who were much in my company.
This was harmful to some artists—those whose job ill fits in
with periods of waiting and obscurity. With regret, I dissociated myself from them, so they should suffer no more

* *I had published then* la Lampe d'Aladin, le Prince Frivole *and* la
Danse de Sophocle, *three nincompooperies.*

from a rhythm of existence which was bringing them but the disadvantages.

There, another chapter off the track, up a side road. The same, if I am translated without the force of the original engaged in it. Writing just as I please, with no guide (at least I boast about it) I get lost. That's the excuse that the translators offer, if they in turn go astray. But nothing dogs them but professional conscience, admittedly a force, but a feeble one, for it incites many men to disobey it. In my opinion it is insufficient unless some still stronger force resides in us and condemns us to hard labour.

# Of the Pre-eminence of Fables

FROM the fact that a truth may take diverse forms, men make much muddle, and each time they take note of something given as true they are astonished there is so little connection between what they see and what they are told about it. Our opinions are based on matter which in us and in others gets deformed. Our readiness to mythify and accept myths is incredible. A falsified truth is soon gospel to us. To it we add something of our own brew, and little by little a likeness is formed which bears no relation to the original.

Experience teaches us to be wary of this deformatory quality. Recently, at Villefranche, having allowed myself to be cradled in a dream, to be precise, about a fabulous luxury liner on which a cruise cost ten million francs and all its tourists heavy with pearls, I agreed to go to see it and found merely a pleasure steamer just like any other, its cruises costing only one-tenth of what I was told, a fleabite to an American purse. The passengers were of a class corresponding to that of pilgrims to Rome—all reverends and their worthy families, an assembly far removed from the fantastic picture which my various sources of information had built up.

While on board, I reflected on the ideas I form of politics according to what goes the rounds about them, and I thought too of foreign governments who get just as wrong about ours as we get about them. It is very hard indeed to cure oneself of such deceptive, distant visions. As it travels, one's anecdote changes sex, height, age. It goes the rounds from mouth to mouth, from ear to ear. It can happen for it to get back to one so worked up that we just don't recognise it any longer.

⌐What is serious is that this transmogrified shape of things assumes its own life. It replaces the original shape of things in the amalgam of time and space till canvas supplants model and the original ceases to convince us it is real. We come to hate it for not adapting itself to our mould, for obliging us to make a new casting.⌐

In the way in which any act is accomplished there are always prime movers which escape us and yet determine its singularity. It is this singularity which strikes one and that we need no special study to observe. And there you have fables on the march. As many different fables as there are witnesses. Assuming the force of art acts are turned to fables by rhapsodies, by the troubadours who sing under our windows. Such is the movement of History, and we should get the surprise of our lives, were a miracle to allow us to spend but a minute with Socrates or Alexander.

Most likely the destruction of the library of Alexandria, in which so many secrets had been accumulated, is not to be ascribed to the mere folly of a leader, but that person was merely the tool of occult forces which were determined to put the brake on man's knowledge and reduce to base again.

Not a day passes but I have proof of the monsters born of our encounters. Our own legend should instruct us on the inexactitude which leads the world and the danger that inexactitude would present in the poor agreement of the nations, were it not that that poor agreement arose from a disorder which nature requires in her constant concern to produce the slaughter on which she stuffs herself.

That is why for all our longing to resist fables, we are seduced by them. They grip us and sweep us away. One has to recognise in them a reflection of the pulse of the universe. Were the correspondence exact, platitude would result, and Nature disapproves of that.

When a minister innovates a system of order, the banks which did not give him credence and gambled against his programme reproach him with ruining them and look upon

him as an enemy to be conquered and achieve this, collaborating with the imbalance which for a moment threatened.
Fable is swift to sprout on the ruins of a monetary initiative.
It obliges gold to withdraw its backing. For the fables of the
Stock Exchange are not among the lesser ones. Fortunes go to
the scaffold and are shattered on mines, sugar cane, and
non-existent petroleum wells.

The radio makes it feasible for us to trap a phenomenon of
the fabulous world. It gives the human voice the speed of
light, so that it reaches us from afar more rapidly than it
reaches those who hear it close to by the intermediary of the
slower sound waves.

That evening when the bells rang out for the liberation of
Paris I was with the Claude-André Pugets at the *Palais Royal*
and we were able to listen to Jacques Maritain, who from
New York told us what we were living through. His scene
however was not at all like ours. His was a sublimation in
which he compelled us to believe. And he was right. New
York was merely immediately substituting historical truth for
our truth. Thus with the storming of the Bastille, which was a
much smaller event than the stories make it (less than that of
the Tuileries). Louis XVI himself was actually quite
unaware that it happened. He was out coursing where today
runs Méchain Street, near Arago boulevard—the boulevard
of the original guillotine. Nevertheless, we still celebrate the
taking of the Bastille.

Unfortunately, whereas historical deformation tends to
magnify, that which concerns us rather tends to depreciate
and abase. Yet I think that in the long run this piling up of
degrading inexactitudes at least raises the pedestal on which
one's bust stands. There is still a sort of truth in them. The
more so since inquisitive minds insist on discovering exacti-
tudes. The new fables which they extract from the old are
added to them and we end up with our busts painted in
bright colours.

*          *          *

⌐If what every guest at a table imagines about our souls could be changed into the object, we should have to fly. We hang on merely through ignorance. The sudden discovery of the misunderstanding which groups us would cut the ground from under our feet. We should have nothing left to stand on. All we could do would be to lie down on our bellies and discourage each other to death.⌐

On the other hand, boon companions put many a thing right. Yesterday Jean Cocteau and two others, both very old friends, met after long separation. Nothing in our bearing or works to match us up. And yet we all three revel in the fluid of friendship, far richer and more salubrious than any understanding born of habits in common or like bent. The wife of one of these two friends made the observation that our mutual understanding came from our triple indifference to gossip, from the pleasure which the success of the other two afforded each of us, also from inaptitude to envy and a gift of listening as great as that of talking.

That fluid of friendship was more important then any of our differences or whatever any of us thought of the others. When the talk turned to our various fables, one of the company laughed and said that at bottom they were caricatures of us, but we should really find pleasure in recognising ourselves in them. He declared that I do go to rather acrobatic tricks in my efforts to vary and chop up my line, hence it is fair to depict me as a tumbler. He said that he himself, being a Marseillais, was rightly treated as a man of bowls, while the third deserved being treated as the darling author of the newspaper kiosks, his books being the only ones sold in them.

Our friend from Marseilles justified the fame of his native city. We marvelled to discover that he found quite simple the geographical fables which his Marseillais temperament made him admit. He added that folk would be really taken aback to know we were foregathering like that, they would detect some sort of wire-pulling in progress, whereas though we never stopped our chin-wagging, it was all without a single word about other people's business or even our own work.

The same evening, these two friends suggested taking me off to a larger party. But this I declined, holding that it might get us on to cross-roads, and saying I preferred not to stir up the lees. Such large parties do indeed degenerate into photographs and the gossip columns of the press—such as the paragraph in a Riviera newspaper when Sartre was finishing *le Diable et le bon Dieu* and I was beginning *Bacchus*. In this particular snippet one learned that we were collaborating on a play about Werther. A good transformation for Luther! Subsequently we read a whole article in which we learned that this alleged collaboration of ours should lead us to make a study of Werther's despair and suicide.

I rather think it is in *l'Ecole de la Médisance* that a certain phrase whispered at the extreme left of the stage is passed from lip to lip, to become unrecognisable at the other side.

It is rare for anybody to get a story from one and not spin it out a bit, embellishing it, changing its point and its conclusion. History is always on the prowl and it is not rare some years later for an anecdotist to relate the same story as his own experience. Politeness of course then counsels us to accept it as mint new.

At a dinner at which Oscar Wilde was present, Whistler had just told a good story. Wilde said he was sorry it was not his. Whistler said: "It soon will be."

When I tell what I have seen I am accustomed to being told that I am making it up and I am also used to reading words ascribed to me which never passed my lips. For if anything said is malicious, the author shifts the burden of it to my shoulders, drawing down on me the resultant animosities which he would rather avoid. But such gambits are trifling compared with the terrible maze of inexactitudes in which the world tangles itself. And daring indeed are those who would attempt the disentangling. We know that so-called historic words ("last words") were never spoken.

Does it matter? They are characteristic of the characters concerned and without such *dicta* those would be very hazy
figures, their outlines would quite disappear.

\*          \*          \*

Eisenstein told me how stills from his film *The Battle*ship
*Potiomkin* ended up in the Soviet Admiralty as documentary
photographs. Without mention of his name, of course. When
the film was shown at Monte Carlo, Eisenstein received a
letter: "I was one of the sailors who were to be shot in your
film scene." Unfortunately, that episode was a complete invention of Eisenstein's, just as was the Odessa steps sequence,
in which subsequently so many of his compatriots claimed to
have all but been massacred. One is always coming on fables
taking the place of reality. They are the tea-cake into which
our common daily bread is transformed. Vain any attempt
to foresee how this will ever be, by what alimentary canal
what is enlarged, what guyed, and he would be a foolish
fellow indeed who essayed to invent a fable and plant it on
the general mass of people. The same goes for all those little
stories which spring up and go the rounds. Every day sees
the invention of perfect ones, but never with an author's
name. One might think it is the pollen that produces them.
The celerity with which they spread is staggering. Likewise
false reports. They simply gallop. Whereas a man can wear
himself out trying to disseminate the truth, and still fail.
Likewise too phrases which in a flash become public property.
La Fontaine's are many, those of Shakespeare legion. This is
what made a certain old lady from Scotland who had never
seen Hamlet remark as she came away from seeing Sir
Laurence Olivier in the title role that it was: "a decent play,
only o'or many quotations in it."

\*          \*          \*

It is in fables that falsehood acquires noble rank. They

should not be confused with tittle-tattle. In the really chimerical there is grandeur. Without it, Pegasus would never charm us or the sirens, and before telling me a story about animals a child would never have said: "This was when animals still talked."

*       *       *

Nothing more comical than our century's conviction—having a bad conscience, as Sartre says—that it constitutes a sort of apotheosis and will never be ridiculous like an old film. Youth never thinks itself old. Yet it will be goaded with questions by another young generation, which will fall into the same error, mocking it as they nudge one another—was it really true that on the high roads there were actually pumps out of which people got petrol and did people really think they were travelling fast and did they really gather together in cellars and dance to a sort of trumpet and drums?

Most likely the science which we think is reaching the heart of things will then have turned into the fabulous and Einstein will be just as pretty a story as Descartes or Erasistratus or Empedocles is today.

Poetry no doubt has less likelihood of getting lost in its intuitive fables. The Montaigne who called philosophy "sophisticated poetry" was right to claim that Plato was merely an illogical poet and that if he does reach a pinnacle of the idiotic when he defines man as "an animal with two feet but no feathers" he also declares that "nature is nought but enigmatic poetry."

The man who dared stand up against fables would come out well scarified. Fables are carapacious things. They are also female progeny of the invisible. There is a whole troop of them sent by the invisible to confuse us properly, and, what is more, they all know their job.

In my opinion the mythologist is to be preferred to the historian. If probed deep, Greek mythology is of greater interest to us than history's distortions and simplifications, for its parts make no claim to relate to reality, whereas history is a mixture of reality and lies. The reality in history turns to falsity, but the unreal of the fable to truth. In a myth lies are impossible, even though one may argue about this or that of the labours of Heracles and question whether he did it all from love of Eurystheus or from servility.

There is nothing to be astonished at in the sun begging Heracles not to shoot and being so grateful to him for not doing so that he gives him his golden goblet to cross the seas in. One accepts the final pyre, the bloodstained tunic, the seed ejaculated over Deianira by Nessus the centaur, one admits Heracles dressing as a woman and Omphale as a man.

Myths have knottier and deeper roots than history. When we learn that the Danaides invented a machine for drainage it is marvellous to see it develop into a torture.

The voyage of the Argonauts holds me more than any America-discovering excursion. I do not imagine that golden fleece to have been aught but Medea's hair, a fact beyond the comprehension of Jason and his companions. I prefer the crimes heaped on Medea, making her out a poisoner and fateful woman, and the discovery that it was none of it so, to the uncertainty about the culpability or innocence of Catherine de Medici.

Just like Balzac's families do, becoming real, or those of *Fantomas*, in which the carelessness of the authors constantly accords Fandor new fathers and mothers, the least detail of the families of the gods fills us with enthusiasm. That is all related to myths, which is how the book delighted Apollinaire and myself. The authors wrote to us one day to say that tucked away they had less outrageous books. We took note of the fact. They, as a matter of fact, were ridiculous, but their authors valued them more—because of their realism.

At school, history books furnished us with a stuffing of insipid fables, whereas the legends of that through and through invented history prompted us to look for the original springs.

They are the supreme point of fable. I marvel at their seriousness, for Heracles, after killing his master Linos with a sabre crack over the head, was acquitted by his judges because Linos had been about to chastise him and hence he acted in legitimate self-defence. No moth ever touched this wonderful purple cloth into which Greece wove her aristocracy of the invisible!

Let us acclaim them as truer and more intelligible than dry events which our daily paper shows us to have been troubled in some incomprehensible way. Unless of course a Michelet, or at least an Alexander Dumas, turns them into fables.

\*      \*      \*

The man who enjoys fables will never defend himself sufficiently against the shafts of their eyes. As many foundations are here needed as for any earthly reality. Lao-Tze accused even Confucius of world levity. As he emerged from his room, Confucius would tell his disciples that he had "seen the dragon."

The famous stele of young Septentrion who "danced three days and died" does not immortalise a young dancer of Antibes. It indicates the *mistral*, a wind which blows either three days, or six. The inscription is votive. An inscription of gardeners at last on the fourth day able to resume their work.

The severity of fables is due to their branches springing from one seed. And as we have fixed on Heracles, Augias needed have only one dirty stable, and it was quite unneccessary to divert two rivers. But had not that cleansing become one of Heracles' labours, we should never have heard of Augias. Cerberus would have remained no more than a watch-dog which its master lost and Heracles found again for him, had Heracles not gone down to Hell to look for it and there promised Meleager's shadow to marry her sister.

I

Chesterton was right when he wrote that Jerusalem was a small town with great ideas, whereas a great town has little ideas.

There is a square at Verona where fables are incarnate which is more living than any in which monuments to the dead are erected.

# On a Cat Story

*To be not marvelled at, but believed.*

AS far as I know, Keats' cat story has never been written. It has been passed down by word of mouth, changing as it goes. There are a number of versions about, but the mood is always the same. A mood so subtle that I wonder if that is not why the story better fits speech, with its leisureliness, than the pen, which is impatient.

These are the facts: Keats was to go to the village of F. to lunch with a friend who was the parson there. He had to cross a forest. On horseback, he lost his way in it. Dusk made the labyrinth inescapable. Tying his horse to a tree, he decided to wait for daybreak, and try to find a charcoal-burner's hut where he might shelter overnight.

While he was wandering round, afraid to go too far out of sight of his horse, and taking care to blaze a trail wherever he went, he noticed a light.

He made his way towards that light. It came from a sort of ruin not mentioned by any guide book, that of an ancient amphitheatre, a Coliseum, a confusion of arches, steps, tumbled stone, collapsed walls, gaps, brambles.

The light, which was very peculiar, quivered and lit up the dead amphitheatre. Keats went close up, slipped through a gap past a pillar, and peeped.

What he saw pinned him there with stupefaction and terror. The auditorium was occupied by hundreds of cats, side by side, like the crowd round a Spanish arena, they were milling about everywhere, miaowing at the top of their voices. Suddenly he caught the sound of miniature trumpets, and the cats were motionless at once, their phosphorescent eyes turned to the right, from where came the flickering confusion of light and shadow. The light came from torches, carried by fifty jackbooted cats, heading a procession of other cats, magnificently clad, with cat pages and heralds trumpeting, cats carrying banners and cat standard-bearers.

The procession filed right across the arena and began to wind back, when there appeared four white and four black cats, with cocked hats and swords, they too, just like the others strutting on their hind legs. These four were carrying on their shoulders a little coffin on which lay a small golden crown. Behind this came more cats, two by two, bearing cushions on which were pinned orders, the diamonds of which sparkled in the light of the torches and flashed in the moonshine. The procession wound up with drums.

Keats told himself that he must be dreaming, he had fallen asleep on horseback and this was a dream. But dreams are one thing, reality another. He was not dreaming and he knew he was not. He was lost by night in a forest, he was the witness of a rite of which no man should have seen anything, and he was afraid. The moment his presence was discovered that crowd of cats would rush out of the amphitheatre and tear him in pieces with their claws. The heralds trumpeted, the standards fluttered, the coffin was borne, all in a silence made painful by those arrogant little trumpets.

After one turn of the arena, the whole procession moved away. The trumpets died down. The lights were extinguished The crowd of cats left the tiers of the amphitheatre. Many of them leapt out through the breach in the wall into which Keats now made every effort to efface himself. The ruin became a ruin again, with only the moonlight to occupy it.

It was now that a much more dangerous idea than the scene he had witnessed came to Keats. It was that *he would not be believed.* This was a story he would never be able to tell. It would be classified as a poet's falsehood. Now, Keats knew that poets do not tell lies. They bear witness. But he also knew that it is believed that they do lie. And he became frantic, at the thought a secret like this would remain his property, that he would never be able to relieve himself of it, sharing it with other men. A catafalque of loneliness.

Shaking himself, he went back to his horse, resolved to leave the forest, whatever it cost him. He then succeeded in reaching the parsonage, where he was no longer expected.

The parson was a very cultivated man. Keats had great respect for him, considering him, indeed, competent to understand his poems. He told his story, but without referring to the amphitheatre of cats. The parson had been in bed, and had got up again. The parson's valet was asleep. The parson laid a meal for Keats. Keats ate in silence. The parson was astonished to find him so distracted, and asked if he were not feeling unwell. Keats replied that he was not, but admitted that he was under the influence of a worry, the cause of which he was unable to tell. The parson gave him a friendly shake and said he certainly must explain what he meant. Oyster-like, Keats wriggled, but in the end the parson got him to give way, for once his guest had admitted that his anxiety was that he would not be believed, the parson promised to believe him. Keats was not satisfied with a mere promise, but made the parson swear over the Bible. This however the parson could not do. But he did declare that his promise as a friend was really quite as good as the oath of a priest.

"I am all ears," he said, and lay back in his armchair, smoking his pipe.

Keats was about to tell, when he thought better of it. Fear overcame him again. The parson, now very interested, had to let him have his way and say nothing, in order to free his tongue. But at last Keats closed his eyes and told the story.

The parson listened in the gloom, the window open on the stars, the fire dying down. Keats described the ruin, the strange gathering and the strange happening. From time to time, he opened his eyes, to shoot a glance at the parson, who throughout kept his eyes closed, puffing away at his pipe.

Then it happened, just as sudden as a clap of thunder, without either Keats or the parson really grasping what was taking place. Keats had got to the procession, the torches, the trumpets, the pennants, the drums, and was describing the costumes, cocked-hats and high-boots. "Four white cats," he said, "and four black cats, were carrying a coffin on their shoulders. On the coffin lay a golden crown."

He had scarcely got these words off his lips when the cat which was sleeping in front of the fire arched its back. Its hair stood on end. "But that means I am now the king of the cats," it cried out in a human voice, and leapt out of the window.

# On Memory

WERE it possible for the contents of our memory to emerge from us and materialise, the world would certainly be in a clutter. How astonishing that so much junk should find room in our brain, the more so since fresh memories are of such feeble stuff that they collapse, while old ones, being tougher, trample them into the ground. If an old one comes forward, we see clinging to it the soil from which it has been torn. That is why I am always hesitant about writing my reminiscences. Memories or dates would get tangled and so intermixed that perspective would be lop-sided and nothing would hold together.

In dreams, wrong perspective is like that which art determines.* In memory our rules no longer apply. Dead and living alike move together on an artificial stage under fatal lighting. The stage is free. It creates scenes, it builds up, it intermixes, it offers us shows far more truthful than realism, for that is merely a one-plane pandering to our limitations. It delimits us, turning the time-scale upside-down. Our nerve-ends float like seaweed fronds in nocturnal waters and join hands without our will. We live a life freed from our fixed tracks. As we waken, supervision comes to life. Memory exposes its wares, but all it can offer are a few fragments, and those are given grudgingly.

---

\* *Dreams are so instantaneous that in one second one can dream the equivalent of a Proust novel. For that matter, Proust's works are closer to dreams than the accounts of dreams we read. It has the limitless number of characters, the fluctuating plot, absence of chronology, cruelty, the fateful, the idiotic, precise scenery and the same "all's well that ends well".*

As far as I go, memory makes a great effort to understand what I do. When it listens to me, it is to reply with cunning and surprise, as when a name escapes me and I harrow my memory till just to keep me quiet it tosses me the morsel I want.

*     *     *

I don't know what philosopher it was that said: "We walk the roofs of Rome." That is what we experienced at Alexandria, where the new town is built on the old.*

It hovers like a memory. One suspects some presence rather like a phantom memory, which we feel to be there, without being able to fill in the application form for it. Was not Nero's palace, consisting of nearly four thousand rooms, covered by an artificial hill on which baths were erected? Had not Rome forgotten it when there was a subsidence and Michael Angelo broke his leg on a memory? That is, on the Lacoon group which used to ornament the roof?

Whole periods of our lives are buried away. It only needs a subsidence, a name to trip over, for four thousand rooms and a thousand mobile vocal statues to appear with it.

The tomb of the Egyptian monarch Tut-Ankh-Amon was *a memory*, in the sense that the everyday objects of his reign were tumbled together, broken, pressed, compacted, inextricable and inexplicable, in a minute cellar, from which without sorting out their confusion the dead man was to reconstitute them for his use.

It was impossible to get inside that cellar. Ten years were

* *The squabblings of Egyptologists prove the discredit from which some excavation has suffered. The accidental death of the best of our young Egyptologists, Alexandre Varille (killed on a French highway), is an example of the defence of the unknown, on all registers. The mockery of official Egyptologists for Varille's work L'escalier est dans la concierge does not solve the problem. The stairs being as much in the porter as vice versa. I had the proof of this when my own porter no longer brought up my letters, saying it was useless to do so as there was going to be war. Here the stairs were definitely in the good concierge, preventing her taking the stairs.*

necessary for the remembered objects to take form and ornament a floor of the Cairo Museum, whence my memory sends me them.

Egyptologists wonder if these objects were not copies, whether those we have were the ones actually used by the Pharaoh, or others, copied for his tomb.

One wonders whether the memory of a dream is not made of copies which memory offers us in place of its own real ones. Those it uses for its own shows. There is no doubt, when a man relates a dream he seems to be staging a setting, actors, action, all of which are like the setting, the actors and the action of the dream to the extent to which made up as politician, an artist resembles a politician. Remembered dreams lose their lighting and persuasiveness so much that they bore one's audience when one relates them, for the audience sees but the show. The dreams have faded. They lose their lustre just as an underwater plant does when taken from the water.

When with closed eyes one demands of memory an episode in the room one is in at the moment, memory provides another which is like it, but situated elsewhere. Similarly, when suddenly wakened in a town room to which we have come from the country, we need to take care not to get up too quickly, if we need to go to the lavatory, for what memory provides us with is our country room, so that we look for the door somewhere else, not where it is, and so bark our shins on the furniture. Memory is delighted to see us lose ourselves and bruise ourselves in this way. Memory is also delighted when we give one of those private shows for an intimate friend, letting him think that a scene of a dream was one of our real universe.

I could write volumes about this. I am often the victim of the substitutions and frauds in which that terrible storehouse delights. Only I should have to apply to the places which elude me, and most likely they would only give me information which would make me make still greater errors.

*         *         *

There are people who complain of their memory who find it obedient after injury—for instance, the figures department often opens up after trepanning. This was Matisse's experience. He previously had no contact with figure memory, yet as he came out of anaesthesis, he suddenly had it at his command.

\*     \*     \*

The storehouse of memory is definitely not at my disposal. I have the greatest difficulty in getting anything at all out of it. When I do I am, I repeat, only supplied by condescension. And then the incident which the shadow offers raises a dust cloud vaguely suggestive of the period in which it was set. This is how I come to re-live certain periods—by the aid of a detail with which memory agrees to furnish me. Such a detail returns to the shadows as soon as I have taken cognizance of it, never to appear again except in dreams, where memory is not tight-fisted, but flings wide the doors of its storehouse. It would seem as if sleep is its realm, which, without application forms or passports, it provides with actors and sets and all the accessories which the shows it organises require, we being its King of Bavaria, sole spectator. It offers us shows, but one might think it hates furnishing us with the wherewithal to make our own and then show the stuff elsewhere.

This distant, official attitude which memory assumes, this haughty indifference to whatever we politely ask of it, has gradually persuaded me to keep farther and farther away from its door. I just content myself with piling up in it a present which ceases to be so the moment I see it. Let memory sort it out, classify it, catalogue it, a lot I care! My present slips back into the darkness where I myself shall some day go, and from which only fragmentary images of me will ever be drawn. For that pile of goods in memory's warehouses certainly does tend to damage a lot of what is bundled in. So what I get out is not always whole. Names, faces, actions get chipped under all the bric-a-brac. Often all I get out is a fragment, after which I wear myself out, merely to discover that the other part cannot be found or does not even exist.

It is by reason of such phenomena of memory that we are present at the marriage of time and space, a marriage which engenders a poor perspective, deceiving us and obliging us to go forward in one direction only, unable to withdraw in any other but by this faculty. Sleep wipes out this illusion, opening up to us what would purport to be a world in which our blinkers are removed and at last we comprehend that our human liberty was but that of a horse pulling the plough. But man does not like being made small. He fears even poetry, since it engraves cutting *dicta* on the walls of our cell. Freud's *Key to Dreams* comforts it by covering the walls with obscene graffitti which the eye is used to seeing everywhere about it.

\* \* \*

My memory is never so pleased as when I take no notice of it. That leaves it free to put on a show the same night, repeating it and throwing light on it without my disturbing it. I have no idea what relations it has with those tenebrosities which give me my orders, or if they are beneficent or not. I do not know whether they experience its loathsome lack of restraint. I do not know if they connive. I am rather inclined to think that some memories come out of my own pocket. That they come from a different region, foreign to the work required of me. Work which does not admit them except when it profits by them.

\* \* \*

When memory dozes, it is only a cat-sleep, and I am afraid of its tricks. It lets some ridiculous trifle out of its store and forces the thing on us. Usually, what it thus compels us to accept is painfully and aggressively ridiculous. Does it perhaps do this just to prove its power? It is certainly vain of us to try to get away from the thing, sending it back whence it came, for memory forces it straight back again, seeming to delight in the trouble which the intrusive thing causes, puffing it up and swelling it out till it cuts off all our sunlight. There are folk who find galled satisfaction in this. Spleen and *le cafard* grow fat on it. It is not my style. I should prefer the dingy jetties to fish up nothing but delightful things for me. I find my consolation for the very feeble control which I have over it all by the strength of childhood memories. Afraid of the dark, the disobedient little things fling open the doors and reach me breathless, their cheeks flushed. True, they are very soon made to leave me alone and get back into the shadows. Family albums are evidence of that. Memory seemed powerless to keep them back. They got out in crowds. It would not be the same were I obliged to appeal to my recent memories. Back I should be in waiting-rooms, filling in forms, suffering official rudeness. That is why I renounce them, despite the offers coming in from all over the place.

The only benefit I find in this administrative system is that it manages to lose so many bad memories. One would almost think they are not filed at all. On the other hand, it seems to hang on to insignificant memories, rather in the way in which fragments of lace curtains survive conflagrations. Memories of that sort, which it scorns and does not lock up in strong-rooms, it gets rid of fairly easily. Memory may not know it, but those are the ones I prefer and which delight my heart.

The store-rooms of memory do not only contain what we have stowed in them. They also contain the memories of our ancestors and of the ancestors of our ancestors. There you have the excuse for some disorder and for the irritability about enquiries.

It also happens that memory's office staff mixes up the records and shows us an entirely new event as having been lived by us. This phenomenon lasts a lightning flash of time.

It is rare. The fact that it is merely a technical hitch is revealed by the insignificance of the events which we are shown, coming as it were out of the store-room before having been stored in it.

Sometimes it happens that memory furnishes us with what we apply for but minus its context, by which I mean, without an additional detail which alone would make it usable. For instance, we are served out with a face minus its name, or the name without the face which would throw light on it. We are not supplied with a familiar name in the instant when we really need it to introduce A. to B. We are left gaping when somebody asks us if we recognise them, insisting on some proof, and perceives our discomfiture, particularly if we are quite sure we do recognise them, but the name slips us.

Our inability to get a particular thing out of the store is no hindrance to the gap in which we would place it being tangible enough or our being quite well able to distinguish its outline without being able to fill it. The gap is as precise as the rectangle of clean space marked out on a dirty wall when a picture is taken down, or the imprint of a piece of jewellery in the velvet lining of its case. Velvet and wall alike are evidence of an absence. They can neither name it nor depict it. There you have one of the stock tricks of the office staff of memory, quicker at dishing us out with the wall or the velvet than the picture or the piece of jewellery. Not to speak of a stage set minus the artist, a word without the lips, a place devoid of geographical position. I am speaking of the shape of the space, of a space which has form, of a space within space, of a space which irks us because it marks out the contours of what should be there, though this ghost of an object refuses to tell us its name.

*　　　*　　　*

I avoid touching on such common phenomena as those of penthotal, hypnosis and psychoanalysis. Memory's store-house has not an excessively high opinion of these artificial devices for tricking it. It lets very little out, hardly any more than it would without the device. It is even amused by it, and lets out things required by falsehood. That is how it is that husbands who have insisted on experimenting with penthotal have heard their wives confess sins they never did commit and acts of turpidity beyond their powers. I shall be countered with the argument that those things were in the memory because the good ladies would have liked to be guilty of such turpitude and to have committed such sins. But that has nothing to do with memory. Those were things out of another store-house altogether.

*       *       *

Le Mémorial de Sainte-Hélène provides us with facts regarding the procedure of memory's office management. The Emperor keeps on asking Las Cases why he never told him earlier about the need for this or that reform. And Las Cases puts in his applications. What he gets out are memories of an Emperor who was unapproachable, ever out of reach, deaf to the advice of those about him. But this Emperor, being now cut off from the world in Las Cases' company, now finds it impossible to imagine a Las Cases incapable of approaching him and telling him something.

*       *       *

There are ruins of buildings so impregnated with ideas and acts that one would almost claim there was a memory in them, and that memory has helped them survive. This is particularly striking at the Parthenon, which I first saw in 1936, full, moreover, of schoolboy mistrust. I got there at mid-day, amid an implacable silence. The first thing that struck me was that that silence was eloquent. The language it spoke was unintelligible, but it certainly spoke it all right, and I observed that that mode of speech came from the columns. There is pinkish fire in them to this day. This fire they emit, exchanging memories

There are other columns which are dead and do not speak without our intervention. Those of Sunium, for instance, the temple of which is a skeleton corroded by the brine of the sea. The columns rear up like so many rods of piled cigar ash. They are silent, even though the loud-speakers which in 1949 surrounded them did lend them a sort of oracular organ. Lord Byron's signature made itself just heard there, a minute grasshoppery voice. But compared with the ruins of the Acropolis at Athens, Cape Sunium's ruins have no memory.

*     *     *

How I have digressed! I was anxious to make myself worthy of the learned man to whom I dedicate these jottings. Impossible. I proffer him my apologies. The excess of contradictions must surprise him, even though he be an adept of the theory of contrarieties and assure me that poets first discover, enquire but later.

How I should like to put together precise blocks of stuff and turn them into a grand temple to Minerva! A temple in which I should not go in fear of her terrible helmet with the blue eyes, like a 7. But all I do is blindly pile up blocks of unreason. I surrender myself to the delights of disobedience. I get utterly absorbed in it. From time to time I do get a bit tired of my disobedience. Then I obey. Perhaps the periods of obedience will throw a little light on the others, my blocks of dereason will prove to have decipherable markings on them, much as one finds dates on the blocks in the Eleusinian chaos.

It would have been my ideal to have a writing-desk and to seat myself at it at fixed hours. To find the right phraseology for a speech. To conduct the speech after my own fashion. Not to get into marginal digressions. Not to lose my sense of direction. To find it in the starry heavens.

All that is beyond my strength. I aspire to it but do not know it and never shall.

Alas, to get down into my tenebrosity, why, my dear René, have I not your deaf lantern, why, my dear Sartre, have I not your power to grip? Why cannot poets be what they ought to be: teachers. A poet is entrammelled by thousand superstitions. In Sartre there is total absence of superstition. He can go under any ladder.

In the *Saint Genet* work (foreword to the *Complete Works of Jean Genet*) we are present in a theatre in which, for the duration of five hundred and sixty-three pages, Sartre, a linen-wrapped surgeon, mask on face, opens up a Genet anaesthetised on the table. Takes the machinery to pieces. Then puts it together again. Then sews up the gap. And Genet breathes, free again, and when he wakens will not suffer, though when he leaves the operating table, he leaves another Genet behind, after which that one too gets up. The one will have to conform to the other, or show a clean pair of heels.

In a dream Sorbonne, Sartre improvises a monster thesis such as not one of his fellow writers would dare tackle. He moves his chess pieces so ruthlessly over the chequers of our time that he stalemates. He wins and I lose. I move defensively and the least breath puts me out.

*          *          *

P.S. In my book *Opium* I have just come upon a case of memory releasing its stores at one sign, whereas another sign would never have obtained it. A sort of *Open Sesame*.

One day, when I was on the way to Henner Street, and passed by La Bruyère Street where I spent my youth, at No. 45, a town house of which my grandparents occupied the second floor, while we had the mezzanine flat (the ground floor was completely given over to a class room opening on to the courtyard and the trees of the Pleyel garden), I resolved to get the better of the fear which in that deaf, blind street had always made me run. As the carriage doors of No. 45 were open, I went in under the arch.

With astonishment I examined the courtyard where I had divided a summer between my bicycle and making a Punch and Judy show, when the *concierge*, all suspicion, stuck her head out through an attic window which had once been forbidden to me and wanted to know what I was after. I said I had merely been peeping at a house of my childhood. "You surprise me very much," she said, and came downstairs and out through the hall to me. She inspected me, then, finding nothing to persuade her it was all right, to all intents turned me out, banging the door of the courtyard after me. And with that distant reverberation she awakened a whole crowd of fresh memories. After that shock, it occurred to me to run down La Bruyère Street all the way from Blanche Street to No. 45, with my eyes closed and my right hand dragging along the railings and against the lamp-posts, just as I had always done on my way back from school. When that experiment did not furnish much information, it suddenly came to me that at that time I was not very tall and so my hand did not touch the same things as it did now. I repeated my experiment, and thanks to a simple difference of height, by a phenomenon analogous to that of the run of the gramophone needle of the rugosities of the record, I obtained the music of memory. It all came back: my cloak, the leather of my satchel, the name of the pal who was with me, the names of our masters, certain things I then said, the tone of my grandfather's voice, the smell of his beard and even the material of which my sister and mother's frocks were made.

# On Distance

*M. Langevin:* But how do you measure
these things?
*Einstein:* These things are not measured.
*Discussion at the Collège de France,* 1923.

OUR senses limit us between this point and that. Sense
of scale is an example of such limitation. We have to
accommodate ourselves. Certain plants and certain
gases happen to extend us one way or other. (Peyotl, or
mescalin, takes us outside our scheme of perspective and
colours, nitrogen dioxide, beyond our scheme of time). And
dreams themselves do, in one second allowing us to live
through relationships as intricate and voluminous as those
of Marcel Proust.

No question, our disobedience to the laws might be
richer than that of conquering sleep and staying up too late
at night, instead of following the delightful way of life of
convolvulus blossoms and obeying, for they change colour,
fading and furling their petals and going to sleep as soon as
night falls. To us, a thousand fields of disobedience are open,
we have a thousand files with which to sever our cells' iron
bars, a thousand knotted ropes by which at risk of broken
neck to climb down. Is not escape indeed the prisoner's
obsession, even at cost of a sentry covering us with fire,
seizing us as we reach the ground, reincarcerating us?

Whip the waves like Xerxes* if you like, address a challenge
to Mount Athos, fire your arrows at heaven like the Thracians,
you will never change the shape of things. Far wiser attack
realms whose indifference will not put us to shame for so
doing, for the act will not be verified.

* *Or scold them like Canute.*—Translator.

132

The pride of painters (and this primarily against the tribunal which judges them) comes from their transgressing the aesthetic laws which enclose them, framework which they break, forcing on us whatever order, accounted disorder, they choose to substitute for the order last established.

It was with such thoughts of the artist's canvas and the inevitability of colours, against which critics bang their heads, frenetic as flies on window-panes, that I conceived the notion also of seeking liberty on a sheet of paper by examining (for better or worse) a theory of distance, a theory the emanations of which I sense and from which I can only find liberation by getting it clear and discarding it. Theory invincible, since to combat it man's armament, for all he imagines it so highly perfected, consists but of primitive weapons.

*     *     *

It is beyond question that Proust perceived true time, the false perspective this assumes and the feasibility of our imposing a new one. But Proust's attachments are too powerful for him to get free,* too much greediness ties him to wild rose, hotel table, particle, frock. Doubtless this is as it should be, since he merely wants to conquer realism. Clinging, as he says, to immediate sensation, he slips back into realism of a different sort, which he limits to a combination of flashes of vision and audition reconstructed thanks to the distorting operation of memory.

* *Proust's three types of action: longing for things from a distance, non-enjoyment of them when possessed, re-detachment from them, to re-achieve enjoyment from a distance.*

*This distantness being Proust's proximity, his proximity has to move things away till they are invisible. Example: "But, above all, the diminution of the pleasure which previously I had thought to possess was due to the certainty that nothing could ever take it from me again. . . . This particular evening the belief, then the fading out of the belief, that in a mere matter of seconds I was going to meet Albertine, had made her almost meaningless, then infinitely dear in my eyes."*

Thus it is a novelist's method that he advocates and achieves. Which does not rule out the possibility of escaping in some other manner, the range of such possible experiments being unlimited. It is to man's glory to be able to conceive things devoid of any features, which does not of course prevent its being difficult to name the un-nameable, particularly if we lack a scientific vocabulary.

In a nutshell, the matter of which we consist is much farther removed from us than any observable galaxy. It is utterly unobservable. Too far off (too close) to be observed. Subject to a law of remoteness which eludes us.

Do heavy and light, short and rapid, large and small and other certainties among the less certain really exist? We have contrived to turn our infirmity into laws. But we still cannot but admit that they may not be universal and that just as between one notion and another laws vary, so these may apply only to our human sphere. I perceived evidence that beyond certain boundaries our legislation would be found astonishing, that it regulates only our realm, that the legislators are our chemists, mathematicians, historians, astronomers, philosophers, biologists and that even if we are not at liberty to express certainty regarding it, we are free to have a hunch.*

It is in this frontier between the visible and the invisible that the whole matter lies. Beyond it, everything is tipped up, and any approaching object does not grow smaller, but seems to stay small. And the small (human smallness); between what concerns me: insects, microbes, neutrons, electrons—and what does not concern me: the whole which we can never see, the frontier is diffuse and uncertain, thereby so

---

* *There are prodigies of figures. Evariste Galois, the Rimbaud of mathematics, who died at the age of twenty (May 29th, 1842), the victim of his teachers, had already written sixty pages which still offer vistas unknown to men of science. "I am a barbarian," said Galois, "because they do not understand me." Also: "I have outlined lines of research which will certainly halt the pundits in theirs."*

much the more alien. On the one hand, a scale of values, heights, weights and measures, on the other, a scale which escapes us because of that distance which is both close-in and totally unbridgeable which preoccupies me.

One should go the whole hog, and, if there is neither weight nor dimensions, one should say there are no distances, and that not merely do the distances deceive us, but further, that they really result from a protective error in our machinery. Just as we have decided (or thought we can take note) that there are things heavy and things light, things large and things small, we have established that there are also things close and things remote and that though in one way this suits us, in another way it also disserves us, for it prevents our following a road which would liberate us from our cell, allowing us to get outside it without getting outside it.

In such realms, despite the distance which separates A from Z, it would be wonderful to be able to use them as we use the alphabet when we form the word azure or Zamore, and suppress the alphabetic distance.

It would be necessary to accustom ourselves instead of "How small it is," to saying "How remote it is," and to believing this, sensing that this distance which seems not to exist, does exist, and that the facts of taking something in our hand and the hand which takes this something are incalculably remote from our thought and our vision. We should then give consideration to an occult measurement which would allow us, not to see the invisible, but at least not to situate it in another realm.

A form of distance still unknown informs us that what is close cannot be distant. This error blinds one to the mechanics of the worlds, where neither the infinitely large nor the infinitely small are a graduated series, but are all one model which tricks us by a feint, by blinkers on our senses, by a secret law of relationships.

\*        \*        \*

For this distant has nothing in common with the object from which one gets increasingly distant. It makes the close thing imperceptible and binds us to the matter all round us, invisible and visible to our sight. It dissimulates for us worlds and worlds of worlds the enigmatic remoteness of which mimics compactness and forces the fable of it on us. It gives us illusions about the appearance of the smallest object.

\*　　\*　　\*

We only recognise the relief and difference of heights in a picture by a mental process which one imagines to be instinctive, but which is not so. Eisenstein once told me that when he was turning his film *The General Line*, he went into a poor cottage. On an inner wall were two postcards, one of Cléo of Mérode, the other of the Eiffel Tower. When he questioned the old peasant-woman whose room it was, she replied that these pictures were of the emperor and empress. She was ignorant both of the new régime and of what the pictures represented. To her, such pictures could therefore but be of the Tsar and his consort.

Certain Indians of high mountain country where neither mirrors nor water-pools are known, recognised other natives in a group photograph, but did not recognise themselves. They asked who "the strangers" were. But they could at least make out that these were pictures whereas there are peoples who cannot even do that, and will look at a photograph upside-down.

The mental operation involved here is indeed rather difficult, whether it is a representational work of a cubist or abstract painting. The mind is used to precision, to having things in focus. Thanks to this, the realistic picture is construed at once, but the mind is not used to the focus of pictures addressed to the mind's eye.

What shall we then say about the focus of perspectives of time and space, for regarding these man possesses only the most illusory and confused notions? To such an extent that,

returning to a town room some years after being there before,
I soon felt as if I had been there all the time and the lay-out
of the place was so much in focus that it could abolish those
years between.

Man soothes himself by a conception of present which is
as false as a reflection in running water. But the flowing
waters of time do determine the ageing of the fixed image
which they reflect. This image, though fixed, is thus in flux
in another manner from the water of time which flows
without taking the reflection with it. This is because neither
is the reflection fixed, nor does the water of time flow, but
this all moves according to laws which elude us.

\*       \*       \*

It is beginning to be audacious thinking to suggest that the
smallest microbes contain a crowd of others and so on. In
1952 a doctor hardly dares claim that he has discovered that
a tiny microbe contains only one other which is still more
minute. What if this doctor guessed, and we too guessed, that
that sort of invisibility all related to our realm, and that there
was another realm which depended on laws which our senses
could not conceive. And yet I consider that this microbe may
not be small at all, to itself, for it is not small and even without
going outside our realm we have here a monster which is not
small, but *distant*. This distant astonishes. But the real distant
which is outside our realm and lies beyond the frontier of the
comprehensible would astonish us still more, were it revealed
to us.

Alas, I lack the professorial facility which would allow me
to pursue this line of research.

But that is not to say that one day artificial senses will not
extend the zone of enquiry of our senses, and my blind-man's
stick then touch the reality of the discoveries of Leonardo da
Vinci or the fantasies of Jules Verne.

Probably nothing ends or begins. Once the concept of
minuteness is rejected, one admits that worlds upon worlds

swarm in all these senses which we designate by the terms immensity and minuteness. That all the worlds are of equal volume (except as far as fragmentary, explosive systems like ours go) and that only our inaptitude to conceive this prompts us to people the immensity with gods and believe that the infinitely small implies a limit.

It is therefore certain that a new conception of distance would abolish the ridiculous notion of the infinitely small having a limit, and that if the notion of small and large were emptied of its meaning, that would make it possible for us no longer to get lost or to come bang up against such phantom ramparts as those of the vast or the minute.

Since any simple communication is already almost ruled out nothing is more difficult to communicate to others than this notion of the infinitely small being without limits, whereas the idea of the infinitely large without limits gains from the imprecision by which so many minds accommodate themselves. It is impossible to make anybody admit that the image contained in a portrait of (say) her (or of course him) holding in her hand a magazine, on the cover of which is this portrait of her holding this magazine in her hand, diminishes in size to the point of vanishing, but for all that is not interrupted and never will be. On the other hand, it is easy to make anybody admit his or her own marvellous body and an apotheosis in which that glorious body is to participate. This notion of a dead point beyond which there opens out a sort of unlimited upward funnel of being is most unreasonable, but it soothes our minds. That soothing action avoids further disquiet, and also enquiries which might abolish others which people hold to be achieved once and for all time.

We are told that an electron weighs a millionth part of a milligramme, that does not mean that it weighs less than the planets. Here in the same manner it is the perspective of this unfamiliar distance that deceives us as to the weight. A mental illusion, just as there are optical illusions.

What resolved me to write this book, after *La Difficulté*

*d'Etre*, is the fact that I am addressing it to the more and more rare people who are read-ers rathers than read-ed and who really study an author's terminology. There is a tendency to slither over the surface of words only and not to grasp that the way they are stuck together is essential to the expression of what they express. The meaning of a sentence is not everything. It is the essence which counts. The inner meaning can only come from a painter's manner, not from what his pictures represent.

If the meaning of the words is upset, what will come of their essence? Yesterday we overheard a lady several times running say *méconnable* instead of *méconnaisable* (*incompreable* instead of *incomprehensible*) without noticing that she was a laughing-stock. There was another (this very morning) surprised to find that the sea was salt. Now, I would point out that those who ridicule this lady are surprised at such instances, but in a domain (our own) on which it is hardly polite to put much emphasis. "It is not in the syllabus" is the phrase which our pupils use to excuse their idleness.

*          *          *

There are several distants which are not at all like the distant which our senses register. Regarded atomically, the time of our system is so dizzy (the telescope merely correcting our eye and the microscope blurring by bringing us close to the distant which does not change its nature by being seen close up) that the details of it disappear, like the blades of an electric fan. From another, totally different, "distant", this whirlwind is fixed, forming a block in which past, present and future become one. Eternity is another term which arises purely from our concept of time. Eternity is no more conceivable than time is. What I mean is that its meaning is a lazy one. In the word *always* there is a notion of continuity counter to the static phenomenon for which as contrast man in his own brevity substitutes the illusion called duration. That is why, without expanding myself on it, I once wrote that time is a phenomenon of perspective to be compared with that of Holbein's death's head. ⌐One therefore really ought to invent a term expressing neither passage of time nor stationary state. But such a term defies invention, because terminology derives from a convention which this concept, being without being, eludes. It is the opposite of nothingness. It is the contrary of life. Doubtless it is very simple, simpler than our own concept, to us poor creatures, at the mercy of centrifugal and centripetal forces, it is inconceivable and inexpressible. Besides, were we to allow of the possibility, we should have against us the double obstacle of science and incredulous folk.⌐

Nothing is either large or small, any more than a thing viewed through opera glasses first one way, then the other, is alternately small and large. ⌐Which does not prevent man's being obliged to be born, and to die. To live, second by second, through events which seem to happen in Indian file, whereas they occur all together and indeed are not occurring at all, because there can be no present in them and what we call past and future are inacessible places which go through us. Which comes to the same as Eddington's *eternal present*. "Events", he said, "do not overtake us, we meet them on our way."

However silly that may seem, nothingness or life, void or fulness are concepts which man carves out like the idols of savage peoples, naive concepts which he opposes to the agony of being lost in it all.⌐

Pride commands some (and whatever it cost) to be something, others to be naught, whereas this naught is as inconceivable as the something, and the something as the naught.

I do not refuse to believe what seems to be. Granted. But, if it exists, it does so in some other way, as foreign to our certainties as, in relation to life, the free and ridiculous magnificence of dreams.*

* *In a dream in which I was walking up and down in the Champs Elysées, facing a fork stuck in the ground between the Wallace fountain and*

And it is this nothing which remains inconceivable to us, to us who are something, whose subjective life is constantly made material in concrete things. This me and these objects which derive from me weigh one down and hamper one. We bump into walls covered with written phrases and to run from one to the other have to clamber through a furniture repository, a regular junk-shop of broken statuary, an attic of childhood with dead croquet mallets and hoops. Why have we not got the ease of dream? In dreams we fly so well that we imagine we should be able to do it awake. But waking, like the three walls which imprison us, we are the victims of an accumulation of things which conceal the fourth wall, which should be transparent and give on to countless other walls (say give on to liberty).

Seen from above, a house is a dwelling-place which I should never reconcile myself to, were it not for use. From higher still, it is a dot. Higher yet, it vanishes. From an aircraft, human existence vanishes before that of man's dwelling-places and cultures. Soon, however, life, house and culture all go.

From still higher and higher, only the motion of our globe will be visible. From higher even than this, that will vanish, just as the motion of the man dwelling on it vanished. It is at this point that one would perceive a solid object seeming motionless, dense, but itself constituted by a dizzy yet imperceptible swarming mobility.

The metaphor is better the other way round. Imagine a microscope the magnification of which steadily increased. First we should see our object, then what the object was made of, then the atoms with their inner gravitation, then certain

---

*the pediment of one of Marly's horses, I told myself that I was doing so while waiting to wake up, then, waking up a little more, asked myself why, thus walking up and down, I did not light a cigarette, as I usually did. I only then realised that in my dreams I never smoke, which cannot be without relationship to the avoidance of cigarette smoking in my plays, which I had always put down to the stop-gap nature of smoking for an actor, an act which should appear neither in the text nor the acting of it.*

among these atoms, then an atom under bombardment, then a bombardment coming to rest, then orbs and starry tracks, then a planet, then a detail of that planet, which would seem to be motionless. Beyond that would begin the sight of what that planet held. Then little dwellings, those who inhabit them, living and dying.

Thus, seen close up, a house does exist, so do those who dwell in it. Seen from a distance, it does not exist, neither do they who live there. Seen from still greater distance, time shrinks like space till it is only a speed which at last moves at that pace at which for the ideal observer it becomes fixed, the speed in his eyes becoming incredible, the centuries succeeding each other at such a rate that after the first scene of continents changing their shapes, oceans invading continents, mountains rising up, islands vanishing below the waters and, nearer, temples and other buildings rising up and falling in ruins, horses, carts, motor-cars moving over the roads, and so forth (all at high speed, as in high-speed films), all that remains of it a little farther on is the sight of a dead world, which had always been so and will always be, while a little further still, even this world will disappear and all to be perceived will be the system of which its elliptic motion is part, while yet a little farther still, this system vanishes, all systems vanish, all seems inert. And nothing more would ever appear again (which would demand a shattering close-up of the eye apparatus) but matter seemingly dead.

*          *          *

And while some thousands of centuries slip by on earth since our departure, a phenomenon of perspective, despite the fact that these thousands of centuries rush away, will put time back in place in proportion to our approach to earth and will re-form the normal perspective of our journey, just as our airman's approach normally reconstructs the house destroyed and makes it livable with all that it contains.

*          *          *

It is of course understood that this distant, so distant from

our own and so different, should not be envisaged when I
speak of the distances which concern aviator, astronomer or
chemist. The distance I presuppose is that whose perspective
functions beyond the mechanics which, even aided by
science, remain perceptible to us. It is no doubt owing to
scientific habits and the historical conceptions science has of
this earth that it is obstinately against establishing any
relationship between that explosion of which we are a crumb
and those observed in our microscopes.

In these phenomena of perspective, the defence of the
unknown is a triumph. *First*, because a man's reply will be
that he does buy an armchair, does argue about the price,
does have it taken to his house, does sit in it, does get up out
of it, does leave it and does find it there again when he comes
back. The instantaneity of all this chain of action will not be
obvious to him except from a distance, which all cancels out
by reason of the fact that the observer capable of observing
from so far off could never do so except with such apparatus
as would bring his sight closer and put human perspective
back in its place (or without this resulting, if the observer is
on this earth and observes other galaxies, or inhabits other
galaxies and observes us). So he will laugh in my face and
tell me that I am mistaken and will equally laugh in the face
of an observer or thinker from no matter what other planet.
*Secondly*, if a man of science developed this thesis, he would
do so in terms and with mathematics which would render it
incomprehensible to any man living his own life and observing
this (already dissatisfied enough at this life being so short).
*Thirdly*, the notion of short and long, of small and large, is
placed in us with a strength, a really brilliant stupidity,
should I say, which are difficult to overcome, except in the
form of speculations which the daily paper easily masters in
the man whose pride from the earthly standpoint it flatters.

*       *       *

Man is less and less ready to accept his limits. He

transcends them in his own fashion, which is not always a good one. For instance, by ultrasonics which kill and threaten to place in his hands a weapon more and more dangerous.

Such gate-crashings beyond our limits authorise us to envisage a structure of the universe very different indeed from that which is our creed, and also to wonder about problems which are neglected because they disturb our peace of mind.

I always marvel at the flimsy comfort in which men of science live. They scorn our ignorance and never for a moment think of the wadding which pads them off from such things as inaudible sounds. Their occasional blindness regarding their own domestic circle or of the canvas of a painter would be sufficient to blot out this assurance that they are able to penetrate the padding which envelops us and inflicts on us frightful errors of moral optics (ethical sight). True, the precision of their field of studies requires them to stop down their lenses.

All the same, even in their own realm, though they do move courageously in that, they remain prisoners of habits which prevent man's getting beyond certain dogmas and certain relationships. For, in their view, if they did venture beyond these, they would run the risk of losing their aura of seriousness, of tipping over into fantasy, or, to be quite frank, into the poetry which they mistake for fantasy. This is certainly what one of them (Henri Poincaré), meant when one day at Mme. Raoul Duval's house, in my youth, he remarked to me that certain subjects of experimentation gave rise to phenomena which were too peculiar to be of any use or enable us to profit in any way by them.* He added that

---

* *The case of Gaston Ouvrieu* (1917). *His case proved (in vain as far as science is concerned) that one would need very little to turn the human brain into a radar apparatus. Ouvrieu could drive a car at any speed with his eyes blindfolded. He could answer questions merely thought by his questioner. It was not a case of mediumistic work, but of a minute fragment of shrapnel in the meningeal region!*

poets "are very lucky indeed", but that as they never had any proofs, they were never believed.

What do these proofs prove? I imagine that it is this reserve, this attitude of circumspection, like that of the Church when considering a new canonisation, that cloisters our men of science and in another place has made me declare that science lags behind and marks time.

⌈Man has always sought in responsibility a confirmation of his own importance.⌋One may observe that all the cosmic cataclysms which have ravaged our earth have seemed to him to have the purpose of punishing one lot and rescuing the others.⌈From this disorder, he makes an order for his own use. Advantage is taken of a disaster by one for the belief⌉ that an angel—or comet's tail—has swept the earth clean and wiped out one's enemies, another believes that he opens up the waters and closes them again, yet another calls Pallas Athene the angel Typhon and he becomes the big bevel-square of the Acropolis. He puts its effigy of ivory and gold in a marble cage. Numerous texts, Egyptian, Chinese, Mexican, Lap, tell us of a cataclysm caused by an angel who plunged half the globe into darkness and on the other face of the earth seemed to halt the sun. Everybody interprets Nature's work in a way which gives man the leading rôle. Not one will resign himself to being merely dust swept by a cyclone. A limited company insists on responsibility because it fears blind forces and prefers to be under the aegis of a court, hoping of course to win the case, but preferring even to lose it rather than accept a passive role.

The atom is a solar system. Struck by the energy of the photon, electrons leap from one orbit to another several times a second. Whereas (says Velikovsky) *because of the immensity of the solar system, the same phenomenon there only happens once in a hundred thousand years.*

It is peculiar that Velikovsky should speak of the immensity of our system and the minuteness of that of the atom,⌈for this immensity or minuteness are solely relative to ourselves.⌋

To the civilisations of the planets of the atom, the phenomenon seems to take place at the same rhythm as ours.

This is logical, cycles following one another and cancelling each other out, which the texts record as but one single cataclysm, the last before that which is to follow (at the same beat) in several thousands of centuries. This auto-bombardment of the system of the atom leaves man a period considerable enough for him to be able to imagine himself in a safe place and grow proud of a process which the succeeding shock will reduce to powder. The world will then pass on to other activities. It will change its structure, discover Americas.

It would be strange were a period between two normal such shocks to allow man himself to cause an abnormal cataclysm without the least relationship to the rhythm of atomic quanta. Were he to succeed in disintegrating his own system by his efforts to disintegrate some other. Which, *entre nous*, is of no greater seriousness.

\*       \*       \*

The auto-bombardment from which, like all the others, our system draws its energy for the constant intermittent scattering of its quanta, escapes such bombardment itself since, I repeat, the atom which the scientific observer believes to be minute is bombarded several times in what a man calls a second, and this bombardment which occurs in our realm at the same intervals appears not to happen except at intervals of thousands and thousands of what man calls centuries.

The feeling of motionlessness will work in what man calls the two senses (large and small). For, if the eye draws near to a system, it will separate out and discover time in the form that our perspective reveals it to us, while if the eye draws away from a system, it will cancel out time and perspective will then seem to the eye no more than a so to speak motionless stuff composed of an organisation of atoms which it no longer distinguishes and the system of which for all the more reason it does not take into account. That is why time tricks our sense of duration in the same way as our sight.

Which is proof that time and space are but one and that it is only our laws which separate them one from another. This tricks us by the same token that a wisteria twining up trellis work with the skill of a snake is taken by the human eye to be inanimate wood.

*     *     *

A proof that time is but trickery is that a vehicle which succeeded in getting out of its own system into ours would see our atomic dust turn into worlds and its own worlds become atoms in its own trail. If it returned to its system, it would have to do so many thousands of centuries after leaving it. But, as I have already said, with the reintegration of its own system perspective would change and there would be that shift of things by which, despite the centuries lapsed since its departure, it would reach its own world in the normal time for the journey. On the other hand, were certain apparatuses to enable it to observe our worlds from its own and close up, that *close up* would remain a *distant* and it would only see them as atoms with continual self-bombardment. That is why man bears within himself, rather confused, the concepts of the immediate and of duration, the discomforts and contradictions of which he experiences without distinguishing their cause.

Time will play the part attributed to space and will become the time of the air-traveller just as, after having ceased as far as he sees it to be itself (his sight being subject solely to the correction of his mind) his house becomes itself again when he draws near to earth, although all the time that for him it had ceased to be itself, while he was up in the air, it had nevertheless never ceased to be a house for those still in it, awaiting his return.

Let who can comprehend. It is the excessive simplicity

L

which hinders our acceptance of this. Man complicates everything by a left foot foremost effect. No doubt the insoluble would seem soluble to him had he the luck which he did not have of starting off right foot foremost.]

I have already noted the phenomenon which seems to distinguish time from space, by which things from which we draw away in space grow smaller and things which have run away from us in time swell to the dimensions of apotheosis which we know as history and mythology. This time, however, is but a form of space, one of those forms of the distant which hoax us, the possession of things which time conveys away from us being more real in our minds than the possession of things belonging to us or imagined to belong to us in space, the object which I touch (registering without according it the importance which one gives to a lost thing) standing out less than a lost object which I recover by the reverse action and synthetic alchemy of memory.

For that matter, it is possible to consider that we are perhaps not even in a system of atoms, but one part of an explosion of the cell of such a system, an explosion which would certainly be an explanation of the dizzy withdrawal of those stars which are getting farther from the earth and that astronomers spend their time observing (the distance at which they observe them also concerning us and allowing the observation of that explosive withdrawal from which we think we escape owing to lack of landmarks and thanks to a general speed of projection which has nothing to do with the mechanism of the celestial bodies). I add that this explosion is perhaps not one that has happened, but is happening; which to us appears stable because we could only observe the dizzy explosiveness of it from the angle of one of those distances which are beyond man's conception, a dizziness which does not exclude a gravitational mechanics based on an established force.

The fault has always been to believe in our smallness which is pointless and in an infinity which is not much better, in our duration which is neither short nor long, and in an endless duration which is like our own. This would make the infinite, the eternal, an interminable proliferation of cells of analogous size and structure, all believing the others to be either smaller or larger than themselves.

⌈If I am here answered that my preceding chapters contradict me, I shall reply that this book is a sort of day-book, that I consider contradiction the very essence of contemporary research and that it is honest not to touch up one's mistakes.

You will tell me that, this false perspective being our own, it is sensible to stick to it, that if our senses are limited, we should resign ourselves to the fact, admitting it and getting from them whatever they allow us, that if man is a cripple, he does not do so very badly with his crippled nature.⌋There is however no doubt that if man did conceive without effort that space-time is a mirage, he would very likely lose his craving for conquests and ruins. True, at the same time he would lose the pluck by which he masters things and builds. ⌈So all is well in the worst of possible worlds. Which does not prevent its being good to submit with clarity about what it is that one is submitting to, and that it is more noble to continue one's task with the knowledge that that task is a vain one. For that matter, it is feasible that everything we undertake is of like valency and the least of our acts plays a prime part in the machinery of it all.⌋

*    *    *

⌈The life and death of men and of worlds remain the great conundrums. It is likely that here too there are perspectives. That neither life nor death count. That all is a mutual devouring, all turning into motionlessness which is continuous catastrophe where the din to us is silence but neither silence nor din count more than life or death.⌋

The mystery of death is in its apparent impossibility since the so to speak infinitely small, the distant things which make us, should never end.

No doubt the infinity of the human body derives from a duration as inscrutable as our distances and (in the form of legacy or decomposition, that should not be confused with poetic phrases like "Flowers grow on graves"*), the body possesses a permanence of the invisible, that eternity the soul of which men try to magnify. Nor forgetting when I speak of eternity, that that length itself has no meaning except by our distress at being short. I should like people more qualified than I am to concentrate on these contradictory matters which should cease so to be in that zone where our three dimensions would raise a laugh.

\*     \*     \*

[Liberation from our vocabulary and system of laws is a work I dare assail under the aegis of ignorance. Even if it is a life sentence, it is still better for a convict to know he is in prison. The knowledge engenders hope, and that hope is nothing less than faith.]

\*     \*     \*

Ah, how I should love not to turn in circles and to be able to orchestrate this chapter. I am, alas, inept but hope it will serve as theme for some erudite orchestrator. I am incapable of the job, for the gift which I possess is the opposite of intelligence. Alas, it assumes an air of intelligence, but is terribly like my stupidity. That is my tragedy. I feel no shame in confessing it. For intelligence is not my *forte*. To me it seems a transcendant form of silliness. It complicates everything. It dehydrates. It is the bell-wether which leads the flocks to the slaughterhouse.

Thus, the more my mind gets used to freedom, the humbler I become, the more am I resigned to my task. I refuse to see a raven, brother to that of Poe's, perched on a philosopher's bust, croaking *What's the good?* at me every second.

\* *Or ironic, e.g., pushing daisies.*—Translator.

A poet is free not to stick to the rails of science. To conquer that *whatsthegoodism*. It is possible both to respect your technologists and suspect their calculations. Are two and two four? I much doubt it, when I add two lamps to two arm-chairs. There have been miscalculations enough piled up, from Heraclitus to Einstein, for us to be able to say that modern science does not know much more about our world than the ancients who held it to be supported by an elephant.

The shorter my path becomes, the easier the notion of death seems to me and the more it seems to me to come down to the normal condition of nullity which was mine before I was born. If a supreme court judges us, I consider that the notions of before and after, arising from our impotence, were judged as much in the void which came before as we shall be in the void to come. Our acts can no nothing about it, to be explained as a small wind rustling dead leaves. The court of men has quickly assumed the place of any supreme court. But one only needs to see the impudence with which they turn their coats for me to charge with sacrilege these earthly judges who would decide the fate of souls.

# On Friendship

I love who loves me, otherwise no;
Nonetheless no, nothing I hate,
But I would have everything good,
Just as Reason would have it to be.

*Charles d'Orléans**

THE journey we make between life and death would be insufferable to me without the warmth of friendships.

Love is still on the periphery of the orders with which Nature endows us. Its wastefulness misuses the pleasure of the act into which, to assure its reign, it pushes all and sundry. It often seems to misuse it against itself, doing so whenever it protects its economy by fruitless love. This great circumspection by which Nature avoids overcrowding, human jurisdiction labels vice. But perfect friendship was created by man himself. It is the supreme creation.

My only politics have been friendship. A complex scheme in an age in which real politics divides men, so that for instance one would never be astonished to hear that Beethoven's Ninth was a communist hymn. Maintaining one's friendships is considered opportunism. They all want you to be in one camp or the other. You are called on to cut the knots of the heart if the ends of the rope are on different sides of their barricades. And yet it seems to me that we defend the cause of solitudes which seek each other. A policy no longer in fashion. Opinions ruin feelings and once opinions

* *The fifteenth century Duke of Orléans, taken prisoner at Agincourt in 1415, was only ransomed after twenty-five years in English captivity. Then 49, he spent his remaining twenty-five years in the deep country, writing poetry, from which these four lines are taken.*—Translator.

diverge, it is anachronistic to remain loyal. For my part, I am stubborn in this and would rather be condemned for the perserverance of my heart than for any doctrine of my intellect.

By misfortune the forces which concern me here disapprove of certain friendships which invade us and disturb their workings, by taking us off our work. That doubtless is why my mourning list is long, why I have been robbed of friends who lightened my journey. Better to introduce prudence into one's relations. Whatever my leaning towards putting the duties of friendship before those of my task, I resist it, from fear of its all beginning over again and of being punished for having neglected my solitude to serve my friends.

Friendship being not an instinct, but an art, and an art which calls for incessant supervision, many incredulous people seek in it motives like those which move them, sex or money interests. If friends protect us against any of its traps, the community rebels, convinced that our friends act thus out of self-interest. Society does not believe in disinterestedness, which to it is a dead letter. Disinterestedness is praised only in animals. In them it is noted as a sort of triumph of servility. And that is the pretext for touching tales and phrases such as "animals are better than we are." One hears the story of the police dog at Biarritz which found itself seeing its little master drowning when it had a muzzle on and the nurse was hopeless, so found another dog without a muzzle and sent that in to do the rescuing for it.

Every day, a poodle waited for its master outside a country railway-station. The man had died suddenly in Paris. The poodle went on waiting, till, after some weeks, he pined away and died. Then the human beings of that district registered their *astonishment* by putting up a monument to the little dog!

I must confess, I find that monument disturbing. I am fond of animals and I do not blind myself to what they can teach us. But the art of which I speak does not govern them at all. They attach themselves to whoever caresses or beats them. Man prettifies them to prettify himself. To every man the most remarkable of dogs. Which gives rise to mutual blinding.

Friendship implies perspicacity. It admits the faults to which love is blind. That is why the friendship of animals is merely love. They deify us and neither try to correct our faults by having the courage to correct their own, or to correct theirs to serve as example to us, whereas that is the height of the art of friendship.

That monument to the poodle is a monument to Tristan, not Pylades.

*       *       *

True friendship knows no quarrels, except serious ones, which reveal a feeling verging on love and imitating its storms.

In the Nietzsche-Wagner friendship, Wagner did not play a pretty rôle. Nietzsche's demands not being satisfied, his breaking off of the friendship and his reproaches drew on all the justices and all the injustices of passionate love. The great quarrel here was all about love, in the sense that Nietzsche wanted Wagner to be his thing, Wagner wanted to enslave Nietzsche. But Nietzsche thought in the realm of souls they could transcend that confusion of the flesh by which lovers hope to melt in a single cry. The difference of material shows at Bayreuth, when Wagner rejects Nietzsche's manifesto for a collection of funds because he reproaches him with not sounding the clarion of appeal with sufficient brass.

Nietzsche's part offers a supreme example of those feelings of loveliness of a soul that the love which leads to marriage would never fill. That soul-passion, alas, was addressed to a feminine nature which the world and its pomps had lured outside the tempest. Péguy's letter to Daniel Halévy (*Victor-Marie comte Hugo*) and the *Cas Wagner* have handed down to us two astounding declarations of love. The slightest grief proves the passion which dictated them.

I wonder whether in Nietzsche and Wagner we should not see a fresh proof what savage ice-cold jealousy the tasks of which we are the vehicles feel. Whether we should not see in Wagner and Nietzsche one of those couples where the invisible would no longer tolerate an invasion which upsets its interests, where it imitated those people who are unable to bear the sight of an understanding which excludes them. For when friendship forms between tempestuous beings, it is difficult for their stormy winds merely to breathe a prompting whisper. The prompting whisper is here in two parts, the two whispers each fearing the other may get the upper hand and the vanquished assume the features of servitude. It is then that friendship becomes identical with love, at grips not merely with its own microbes, but also with the obstacles which menace it from outside.

True friendship does not develop in this register at all. I call it an art because it is constantly questioning itself, constantly correcting itself and because it signs a peace which rules out the wars of love.

It is probable that when I was a victim of friendship my friends were equally victims because I exceeded the register. If not, it seems to me that friendship is admitted by the tasks before the artist (or writer). Indeed, they exploit it. They find in it a means of making better use of us, since friendship drives us to proofs, to believing ourselves that we are working for a merit which renders us worthy of our friends. A means which derails the moment that friendship exceeds its prerogatives, when one servitude added to another jostles our tenebrosity to the point of upsetting its egoism. In *Tristan and Isolde*, apart from Wagner's love for the woman who inspired it, the passionate love he feels for himself dictates a passionate love style. The work exemplifies the couple formed by certain creators, exemplifies the fever ravaging the monstrous combination of which a fever of external origin is merely a screen of invisibility.

\*       \*       \*

Experiment has perfected me in this art of friendship and regarding the pains which it costs us. The meetings which precede the observances should not find their origin in any sudden flash of love, but meticulous study of the human souls involved.

In this way one avoids harbouring explosives in one's house.

Solely friendship can find the very simple glance or phrase which bathes our wounds, wounds we aggravate and deepen with the ferocity of those who, knowing themselves incurable, seek relief in extremity of suffering. Against such wounds a force like ours can do naught but take flight or follow us as we go the whole hog, and take the road to perdition with us.

Friendship does not wish to be inspiring. It does not flatter itself with feeding our fire, with pouring fresh fuel on our flames, with collaboration in a holocaust, or with playing any rôle upon our ruins.

It observes us without febrility. It preserves its balance merely to ensure our own. At least, this is the aspect from which I see its handsome, stern features.

One can guess how much the absence of anything spectacular irks a world so greedy for such sensation and which would just love to have an orchestra stall from which to see us play out our tragedy. If we do not provide it with tragedy, it seeks for things that good understanding dissimulates. It stages the twists of a plot and then if it gets tired of the game it will complain of our calm and run off to more suggestive shows. There is nothing less exciting for the world than our imperturbability under attack. It hopes to witness a slaughter. I have often met people who deplored my reserve in the *Bacchus* business. They expected more than that. Me massacring Mauriac, then Mauriac's toadies massacring me. The basis of the quarrel did not interest them at all. They were only interested in the squabbling itself, hoping that it would eventually bring us all into the dock.

Sometimes our picadors turn their attention to victims whom they count less apt to defend themselves. That is what happened when thinking they had been wasting their time with my play, they swung round against the *Comédie française's Britannicus* in which Marais was admirable. The audience was most enthusiastic about the production. But the world of which I speak wanted to pursue me through his person, and assailed him with sarcasm in the hope that both our curtains would fall together. But they counted without the friendship which attached us one to the other, a friendship which did not involve our personal ethics, either. True enough, there are other arenas too which distract the spectators from their corrida without any final slaughter. They direct their banderillas, their goods and their old hacks against animals less lingering in their death throes.

*       *       *

The group of musicians known as *The Six* is one the friendship of which was an ethic in itself. I was their historiographer. They allowed me to keep my own ideas. That is why, after twenty years, in 1952 we met, still linked together by the same bond. It was one of those little parties which Heugel calls in one capital after another. So far, the blows which had decimated our friends had not yet struck at our group, though even should they do so, schoolboy squabbles would never break it up. Friendship brought us together without constraint of any kind. We flourished each of us according to his bent. Never once of the many times when the malicious angled to disunite us did we take their bait.

My friendship with Stravinsky has been different. That has suffered from a switchback of crises. But just when the world thinks it really is in ruins, I always find it whole again.

*       *       *

I occupy a fortress the sentries of which protect friendship.

That friendship's fortress has housed me since 1949. I regret I must add that it will hold out and it will not yield unless to forces superior because we have no weapon against them. One great thing is that it keeps well away from general manoeuvres. Whenever these draw near, we elude them on the ocean wave, and on board ship friendship's knots are still further tightened. And if I ever have to leave this fortress of mine, to sally out in rash skirmish, when all is over I return to it again and raise my drawbridge, or I set sail.

In this fortress of mine I have found the proof that friendship is triumphant over all the vicissitudes of love, which is the contrary of the love of Triebschen, into which too many contradictory interests stuffed their explosive grenades. What is this I am saying? No, where the very substance of the soul disintegrated. Our metal is well tempered, and I have never seen any possibility of a spoke capable of upsetting the workings of our wheels.

I am not unmindful that such a privilege is costly. I accept the bill, knowing the goods worth a fortune and that one never does really pay the fabulous sums they are worth.

Through the least crevice infiltrate a thousand harmful waves. If we are not intoxicated by thought of immediate success, it is essential to keep away from their tornadoes. Our crude scholastic age, in its own way medieval, with all the marvellous might thereby implied, loves to demolish and to build again. An idolatrous, iconoclastic age. Miraculous, dangerous, it sanctifies the individual—and ruins him. In it one can only keep one's balance in an invisibility the cunning device of which (for I have remarked how much the invisible always tries to compromise us) is to try to convince us that we have reached middle-age and really must get out of the rut.

History demonstrates to what risks over-estimation of the generosity of our adversaries exposes us, for they are always pondering how to exile us. It would be foolish to confound the exile they would impose with that we choose—or think

we choose—ourselves when the invisible really decides for us
and gains from our voluntary exile.

\*            \*            \*

⌈Perfect friendship, that which is not in the least poisoned
by love, feeds on forces alien to those of this study. I insist on
the fact that when those secret forces engage in it, there is
confusion all down the frontier. And if I speak of an art of
friendship, it is to speak of an art in which man is free and not
of one of which he is the slave.⌋

It may be guessed how much this art recuperates me from
the other, how much I congratulate myself that the shades
do not harry me from it. Nevertheless, it behoves one to take
care, never infringing the rules without which the savage
machinery would start up again.

Having confessed to my irresponsibility as artist, I take
care of the responsibilities of my heart. I never let it lie across
my work. There, my judges will say, there is a life whose fire
is extinguished, one of those who are resigned. Well, let me
confess that I prefer these dull coals of mine to those flames
of delight.

A young châtelaine,\* an adopted son, a rare visitor, a
restricted band of us. On the other hand, friendship bowls
smoothly on without those explosive milestones which the
boredom of the western world likes to dispose all along one's
road so that it should not be "dull". The tempo of friendship
is oriental. Perhaps the great mistake of the Orient has been
to have overestimated the value of the West and its hysterics.
It is the Orient that should have sent the West missionaries.

\*            \*            \*

It is customary to confound real friendship with casual
friendship or *camaraderie*,† which is only a rough sketch for

\* *Her unlimited generosity taught me to break with those* meun teum
*concepts which are the fateful heritage of all French bourgeois.*
† *i.e. what we English call "good friends"—see my foreword.*—Translator.

it and was to be the basis of the *Social Contract*. And what is one to say of special friendships? Montherlant and Peyrefitte depict for us the half-light of those sketchy little loves which develop at an age at which the senses are still in limbo and simply do not know which roads are out of bounds.

Being good friends and indulging in little passions all bears no resemblance to the attachments of Orestes and Pylades, Achilles and Patrocles. It is to be regretted that the monks cast suspicion on such ties, destroying those works of Sophocles, Aeschylus and Euripides which would have thrown light on them for us. What the moralists call Greek love, an erotic intimacy between pupil and teacher, had nothing to do with powerful soul links, and if the heroes did exceed the limits permitted, that does not introduce any new incriminating document into the trial. It is the craving for that sort of attachment that feeds wars, since it draws many a man away from a domestic hearth no longer lit by love, for he finds it unthinkable to tear himself away from its dismal ambiance without some patriotic pretext.

\*       \*       \*

I have spent much time with pairs of such friends. The failings of one are added to those of the other. Each thought the other afforded moral support, whereas it was always the supporter who profited. Such couples resist by reason of a disorder which they raise to romantic level. The state of fable-isation which they attain leads them to a scorn of tranquillity. Alcohol also aliments them, till they come to storms which exceed those of the most umbrageous married couples.

\*       \*       \*

There is a really fantastic story I know and I am sorry to be unable to cite the names, for they would be my confirmation about it all.

A certain architect of le Havre, who had a delightful young

wife, was suddenly taken with an irresistible need to dress up as a woman, although there was not the slightest change of sexual function involved. He was no longer in his early manhood and his obsession was merely to dress up as a most respectable middle-aged woman. He achieved his desire with the aid of a woman friend whom I also knew well. He maintained two flats, two cars and had a wardrobe full of frocks which he used to order from dressmakers, actually going for fittings without the *modistes* ever seeing through it.

His fantasy otherwise was satisfied by conversations with friends who were initiated into the secret. "I ought to find a husband," he would say. "It should be a man older than I am, and not one just after my money, either."

His young wife had no suspicion of all this and would certainly have found it more difficult to admit the strange truth than to discover some genuine vice.

The farce went on for five years, after which the double existence began to become a financial strain, forcing the architect to ruin himself, gambling in his male role for that other ego of respectable middle-aged woman into which he used to transform himself.

Finally, he committed suicide—in his feminine flat, stretched out on the bed, but in male clothing, in his hand a letter which read: "I have ruined myself for myself, and so doing I have ruined the wife I adore. Will she ever forgive me?"

There if you like, was a unique couple! Does it not sum up those pairs of comrades between whom there is neither love nor friendship?

\* \* \*

Knowing my contemporaries and compatriots, I sometimes have to warn the young of the what-will-people-say risk that they run in my company. Strange, they are not a bit like those who look for it, what-will-people-say fear merely makes them shrug their shoulders. The others pretend to be afraid of gossip, while by sly tricks they lay themselves open to it, making no hesitation to dirty themselves and us alike, if only they can get notoriety from intimacy with us.

⌠Youth must be respected before all else and as respect is not to be picked up everywhere there is little restraint in interpreting the impulses of the heart and giving them a nasty label.⌡

The least police report proves this. I do not advise anybody to get themselves caught in that sort of thing. Those gentry having in them not an inkling of the subtleties of heart or soul, spread themselves easily in base interrogations and treat those who from sense of delicacy inevitably defend themselves badly, as if they were patients in an asylum. This delicacy of theirs of course is their inculpation. They blush. That is enough for them to be at once classed as guilty and subjected to the shame of medical examination. I knew cases where the unfortunate persons could not bear the insult. They took refuge from it in suicide, thereby providing the police with another false proof of their guilt. Lamentable. Even where there is a leaning towards what our social order deems vice, the victim is full of additional strain through not fitting into the normal pattern and being considered by his family as a monster.

In another case, frustrated instinct ended in the worst. Bullyragged and bullyragged, analysed and analysed, the victim could find peace only in death.

We make no pretensions about reforming the world. That is science's job. Our explanations can only convince the just who are already convinced.

It remains to state the aim of this paragraph. *To talk to those who read me as if we were together in a room.*

I have often observed the least wild of minds suddenly indulge in unseemly stupidities, which get reported in the press. It can do no harm to light their lantern a little. I am of course not trying to defend myself. I know nothing more vulgar than people who defend themselves or those who boast of having defended us. I have great admiration for Mme. Lucien Muhlfeld. One day a young lady called on her and burst out with the words: "I have just been defending you." We witnessed Mme. Muhlfeld show her the door and advise her never to show her face there again.

People do not seem to know that one should never defend those whom one likes, for the excellent reason that those one likes should never frequent the house of those who talk badly about us. If they do, their mere attitude will seal people's lips. I flatter myself that no mischievous tongue could wag in my presence. If I see one about to begin, I leave the table, or the room. Let them unbung themselves without me. And if I am present, let them hold their tongues. There you have one clause of my ethic. And as far as I know I have never been caught napping.

\*     \*     \*

The Walt Whitman business has nothing to do with amorous friendship. It merits separate consideration. Whitman's translators incriminate him by camouflaging him. And of what? Whitman is the rhapsodist of a friendship in which the word *camarade*—comrade—would re-achieve its true sense. His hymn is much more than claps on the shoulder. He chants a conjugation of forces. He is against those very contacts which Gide confesses. It is a pity that in his anxiety to defend a little known zone, Gide has given us merely a sketch. Wilde idealises it with worldly charm, Balzac too, offering Wilde (in the Vautrin-Rastignac dialogue in the Vauquier boarding-house garden the model of the dialogue of Lord Harry and Dorian Gray in the painter's garden, again offers us force in face of weakness, a weakness which explodes when at last Camusot's Rubenpré attacks his benefactor.

Proust pretends to be judge. In this the beauty of his work loses any great meaning. One must regret that his pages on maniacal jealousy do not give us any real light on this.

\*     \*     \*

M

Let us return to the king-pin of our chapter, friendship, untouched virgin of the fables which society foists on it. Men and women alike are ennobled by it, though women are more prompt than men to feel jealousy. Now, in friendship jealousy should never come into it, for this on the contrary consists in the service of feelings foreign to friendship's register. This neither suspects us nor observes, nor does it ever vent itself in reproaches. Its role would seem to be to see clearly for those blinded by the extravagances of love, to aid them in happiness, if they attain it, or in misfortune, if they feel its blows. This said, friendship should be careful how it meddles in love, or its support is in danger of looking like a trick meant to serve its preservation.

I receive many letters in which I am offered friendship. People are astonished to find I do not leap at such platters and reply to their enthusiasm with reserve. Let me answer that. The Chinese have summed up the art of friendship: "Steady with the heart." Which does not mean: "Deprive yourself of using your heart." And this means: "Chalk a circle, don't go outside it." It took me a long time to test out the friendships which suit me. This cautiousness by no means signifies me triple locking my door. That is always open. But it is not the door of my treasury.

*       *       *

Man has been quick to use the word friendship, to caress, to use tender language, till the lovely edifice is in danger of being destroyed by a mere trifle. I take tremendous care of my own—my true friendships, I mean—lest death lay her hand on them, and whenever to my old friendships I do add fresh ones, my first care is always to put them *au fait* about a past which is strange to them. Thus old and new can mingle, with no gulfs between, and the new ones not shouldered aside.

The metal of friendship claims to be non-rusting. I shall cite friends whom others have tried to delude regarding me and who know quite well whether I am capable or not of words and acts attributed to me. That is, if they agree at all to charges being levelled against me in my absence, which should never be, but, alas, is. For my part, I avoid this like the plague, but whenever I set right this tendency to slander I observe that I disappoint the company, who would rather I came tumbling down the chute.

\* \* \*

⌐One should not believe friendship to be proof against the test of the intemperate.⌐ This book records a number of hangovers. I have mentioned a long study which precedes it. In distinction from love, the perspicacity in which it leaves us should open our eyes the moment it goes wrong. But that is difficult because friendship is indulgent and hopes to get over shortcomings. But if such shortcomings seem not really to be such and come from excess of feelings, disorder sets in without one's noticing it. It may even penetrate by chance into the equilibrium of true friendship. No nature is proof against a shock putting it wrong and forcing it into unforeseen directions. When there are no such shocks, that is an accident to be compared with that of the gambler who wins several times running on the same number at roulette.

However, in the end, we begin to be wary. We assist chance so that it serves us without trickery.

\* \* \*

The work of friendship would be too simple if it were quite sure of avoiding the obstacles in the work of our writings, for in them the invisible world alerts its own police. The more reason for managing both one and the other, never mixing the two jobs—and never letting our tasks think that friendship is jealous.

A fortress is almost indispensable to this tight-rope work, so baffling amid the circus rings and parades, the shooting galleries and the acrobatic feats of a big city.

After the fashion of wine, I recommend friendship not to
let its bottle be shaken. For that matter, it disdains to
dissociate itself, be that but momentarily. This is where it
is like the triad, the disruption of which releases catastrophes.
It would rather travel in a party, so, if there is an accident, to
run the risk of a common death.

The Bishop of Monaco tells me that he was responsible for
the death of a young woman in the Languedoc disaster. She
was in such a hurry to go that he let her have his berth. This
is the bishop of a rock where rises a temple, the temple of
Fortune. Not that the bishop was in any way a friend of the
young woman. He was merely doing a stranger a service.
Had he been a friend of hers, no doubt he would have liked
to make that aerial trip together with her.

\*    \*    \*

Friendship is considered vain in an age of haste and strong
minds. What is friendship to the man who would sacrifice it
to a principle? What is friendship in a world which scorns
delicacy of feeling? *I don't care a fig*, as they say. He weeps
best who weeps last.

\*    \*    \*

P.S. I know it is not modesty to talk about oneself. But there
are fine examples of it.\* Besides, this is a book addressed *to
friends*. It will fall from the hands of those whom it rejects.
And it is normal to converse unhindered with friends. The
mechanics which this book submits to its clumsy examination
will ward off those whose attention it rejects. That was how,
after all, I recognised that it was less free to write than I had
thought. I have wound up by this chapter *On Friendship*
because it is friendship that I am addressing.

---

\* *Custom has made talking about Oneself evil. . . . Those are calf bridles
with which neither the Saints whom we hear talk so loudly about themselves
nor the philosophers nor the theologians bridle themselves. . . . Thus let he
who would be known see boldly to it he is known by his own lips*—
Montaigne.

Perhaps the line of my ethic will show through this human disorder, feeling its way in the darkness and putting attentive souls on their guard against the danger of wild wanderings. There are things we are allowed and things disallowed us. I should have liked to write books fine and beautiful. Whoever dictates these to their authors does not poison them. The future, if there is a future, will alone decide about my imprudence. It is true that I should suffer more had I tried to be prudent.

I have never been circumspect and cannot boast of that, because I do not know what it is. I stick my nose into action. Whatever the result. Erik Satie tells us that in his youth he was always told: "You will see later."

"I am fifty," he told me, "and I have not seen anything."

In certain families if some money is put aside for us, it is the custom to say that it should not be given to us, so there should be "something coming" to us, forgetting that something of life is always coming and we are always dying, every single minute, just as much as, some future day, we shall "die".

# On a Manner

## of Living

Keep the morning razor away from your antennae.

*

For movements, respect, from schools, flight.

*

Do not confuse progressive science with intuitive science, the only science that matters.

*

Pay as much attention to your figure and your undies as does a pretty woman. (Of course not those *I* mean).

*

When it comes to blows, be somebody else (Leporello).

*

Al Brown lay himself open to: "You're no boxer, you're a dancer." He laughed, and won the fight.

*

⌐Don't call attention to inaccuracies printed about you. Such things are our protection.⌐

*

⌐Be a standing assassin of shamefulness. Nothing to be afraid of. The blind have it too.⌐

*

A man is either judge or defendant. The judge sits high. The defendant stands in the dock. ⌐Live standing.⌐

*

Never forget that a masterpiece is evidence of depravity of

intelligence. (A break with standards). Turn it to action. Society would condemn it. That after all is what usually happens.

*

Contradict what they call the vanguard.

*

Go quickly slowly.

*

Run faster than beauty.

*

First find. Then seek.

*

Be of service, even if it compromises you.

*

Compromise yourself. It blurs the trail.

*

Withdraw from the dance, discreetly.

*

He who is affected by insults is infected.

*

Understand that some of one's enemies are one's real friends (question of levels).

*

Mistrust the reflex of ill humour, for it is the most stupid of stupid things.

*

Don't be afraid to be ridiculous about the ridiculous.

*

Be a dish-cloth, don't get mixed up with napkins (or serviettes).

*

See luck in miscalculations.

*

The failure of one project sets in motion another.

*

A measure of silliness is indispensable. The encyclopedists are at the bottom of that cleverness which is a transcendental form of silliness.

*

Do not close the circle. Leave it open. Descartes closes it. Pascal leaves it open. Over the encyclopedists, who close the circle, it was Rousseau's victory to have left his open.

*

Our pen should be the radiesthest's pen, capable of restoring life to an atrophied sense, of aiding a sense which has almost ceased to function and is infallible. (The real personality).

*

Don't seek flight in action.

*

Raise the power of the soul till it is as flagrant as sexual potency.

*

Kill the critical spirit in yourself. In art refuse to be convinced except by what violently corresponds to the sex of the soul, to whatever provokes an immediate, unreflected moral erection.

*

Never expect recompense or beatification. Return noble waves for ignoble.

*

Hate only hatred.

*

An unjust condemnation is the supreme title to nobility.

*

Disapprove of everybody deciding on or admitting the extermination of a race not his own.

*

Understand that our judges know nothing of the mechanics of our work and put it all down to caprice.

*

Show what is unconscious nothing but assistance.

*

Do half your work. The remainder will do itself.

*

If the unconscious in you gets obstinate, do not insist, or dwell on it. Turn to some manual work.

*

Avoid any imagination attributing inner work to external influence occult in nature.

*

Consider metaphysics a continuation of physics.

*

Know that our work is only addressed to those whose wave-length is our own.

*

Contradict yourself. Repeat yourself. Most important.

*

What matters cannot fail to be unrecognisable since it bears no resemblance whatsoever to anything already known.

*

Fear hero-worship like the plague. The hero-worshipped will be blotted out. The un-hero-worshipped de-blotted.

*

Written numbers are addressed to a lower level of the intelligence. The politeness of poets is in their never writing down their numbers. The Great Pyramid's expressiveness is due solely to its relationships. In art the supreme politeness consists in only addressing those who are capable of discovering and measuring relationships. All the rest is mere symbol, symbolism being but transcendental imagery.

*

The wall of silliness is the work of art of the intellectuals. To cross it, one needs to disintegrate. But whatever the cost, one must pass it. The simpler your machine the more chance there will be of conquering this wall's resistance.

# Terminal Letter

My dear Bertrand,

Do please forgive this little treatise of "untutored science". It is an exhausing hide-and-seek in which men won't play, preferring their "sports". Which often prompts us to imitate Heraclitus and keep company again with children at their play.

Perhaps we *are* finite and contain finite systems which contain others, to infinity. Perhaps we are all within one of such finite systems (which would be impermanent), likewise contained in other finites equally impermanent. ⌐Perhaps this infinity of finites, one inside another like Chinese boxes, is not the Kingdom of God, but God himself.⌐ If so it is our duty to admit our scale (where living things rise and fall like tadpoles in a jar), and not get lost in heart-lacerating perspectives.

All is fire, all burnt away. Life is the result of a combustive process. Man has invented how to burn and leave lovely cinders behind him. Some still a-glow, too. By these we perceive the presence of the past, partially revealed in true focus. For such cinders (or creative works) depend on human essence which is imperceptible, and not subject to our measurement.

By the fact that these hot coals will be here tomorrow when we are no longer, they may be said to set foot on what we call the future, giving us a vague feeling of fixity and permanence.

The excavations which a medium makes in the alleged future bring forth objects no less disjunct from their context than the Etruscan vases of the alleged past which come up at Ostia as soon as one sticks one's pick in. That is what disturbs us when we stand before the little oracle of Delphi. Motionless, stable, the toes neatly ranged one next the other, it seems to come from the depths of past ages and continue its road, ever marking time with the white staff of a blind person.

It has always struck me as representative of the illusions of all these time-space perspectives. Behind remain an arm, a chariot, a team of four, a *quadriga*. But just as past gestures elude memory, so horses, chariot and arm seem equally witnesses of future gestures. For me, this is a representation of the eternal present, a sketch of this, an astounding little landmark.

## POSTSCRIPT

During my last visit to Greece—June 12th to June 27th, 1952, to verify figures for my *Oedipus Rex*, I had in my pocket your letter on the scale which Pythagoras and China invented, without knowing it, together. Here are my notes on *Oedipus Rex* and my journey.

# On an Oratorio

Jocasta has just hanged herself. The plague is at its peak. Nobody is seen out abroad. Thebes has closed its shutters in sign of mourning. Oedipus remains alone. As he is blind, he cannot be seen (sic) . . .

At Colone, he related: "I did this thing." I remained right in the centre of the room. My eyes could not bear the revoltingly bright light of that chandelier

*Popular Mystery.*

ANY serious work, whether poetry or music, theatre or cinema, requires a ceremonial, lengthy calculations, a structure in which the least architectural fault would put the pyramid out of balance. But whereas in an oriental play or in sports events, figures and architectural detail refer to a code which everybody knows, ours answer to rules which are proper to ourselves and are unfit to offer proof of excellence.

The work on *Oedipus Rex* was not simple. I could not kill ear by eye. I had to be violent, respecting the mythological monstrosity of it. Indeed, this myth reaches us with the same silence that the flying saucers do. Time and space send us it from some planet the morals of which disconcert. I upset Igor Stravinsky's oratorio neither by the play nor the dances. I was satisfied with seven tableaux, all very short, lasting as long as my text, on a stage looming over the orchestra. It would be inexact to say that I was inspired by the Japanese *No* drama, though I did recall the exemplary economy of gesture, all with allusive force, which that offers. I was amazed by the understanding of the craftsmen which made it feasible for me to make the masks. When there was a problem to solve, nothing strange astonished them. I may add that the wars of 1914 and 1940 have cu. gap which authorises the younger folk to be unconcerned ab ut knowing whether that they are doing is new or not. On the other hand, we both did and saw too many things not to be compelled to try some new ones. For if we ourselves are no longer young, our works must be. *Oedipus Rex* dates from 1923. In 1952, it became a ceremonial piece to mark our reunion after so many years passed far from one another.

*Figaro Album* for June-July, 1952.

\*  \*  \*

It was only in Vienna, on the stage, beside a forest of instruments, facing the crowds in stalls, boxes, and galleries applauding Stravinsky across my presence, that I had the real feeling of the mime, which I had not been able to bring to Austria but which had been produced even at the Champs-Elysées theatre without my really seeing it at all. It all took place behind my back. I followed it in the audience's eye. At the *Konzerthaus* I actually saw it at last, all obstacles cleared, free from my own uncertainties, no longer obliged to wonder whether it was running properly. The impression was so powerful every time, urged on by the leader of the orchestra, and upborne by the waves of applause, that I forgot it was a pure concert version they were producing. In my imagination was an audience which had just seen the whole thing in its original form. This impression, I should make clear, was re-doubled since, never having actually seen the show myself, never having measured it except by the broad expanse of shadow or of light spread over the audience by the rise and fall of the curtain, I could believe that the mime and décor had always been invisible, that it was my inward tensions alone that even in the full stage production communicated it to the hall, quite as if I were a hypnotist. Thus Vienna actually did see it—by hypnosis—of that I was absolutely sure when I mounted the stage for the fifteenth time. Only the regrets expressed to me subsequently about the absence of the acting and all Vienna's demands for exact information regarding the real production, awakened me from that state of self hypnosis in which I found myself. So, to make it visible for them, I resolved to put in writing what in the Vienna concert hall I told our audience. But before even the mechanics of its mime, to me *Oedipus Rex* meant: Villefranche, Mont-Boron, Stravinsky and his family, my own youth, and all that of which I speak in the chapter entitled *Birth of a Poem*. It was as if the period which separated that chapter from the one I am now writing were non-existent and I were relating both at the same time. No doubt that came from sensing the presence of Stravinsky on my left, as well as from the fact that memory substituted its own theatre for that in which I was merely the narrating voice.

*       *       *

The reason I am recording these memories as I did for my ballet *le Jeune Homme et la Mort* in *la Difficulté d'Etre*, is that theatre shows evaporate, erode, crumble away. Of not one of the many plays which I have produced have I even photographs left. No, not even a bit of such flotsam of my *Roméo et Juliet* in the *Soirées de Paris*. That was the production in which together with Jean and Valentine Hugo, I invented the use of a black background, with only the colours of the costume arabesques and any stage furniture visible. Red lights edging the outer frame of the stage prevented the audience distinguishing anything beyond that. Servants thus made invisible built up streets and interior walls about the choreographic movements of the performers. I formalised a very intriguing gait for the youth of Verona, Romeo alone not moving according to that exaggerated stylisation. But where indeed have last years snows gone?

*       *       *

The masks in *Oedipus Rex* were fashioned for being seen from below. When viewed on a level they became illegible. They were mostly ovoid, the eyes set at the end of wands for horns. The hair was of raffia. Ridges of cork, wires, excrescences, isolated from the surface, indicated nose, ears, mouths. This was all surmounted by sheaves of corn which ended in red-painted ping-pong balls—what our French *Midi* would call *semble-sang*, "mock-bleed".

\*　　　\*　　　\*

Gesture which never went as far as dancing, hardly exceeding pantomime, was essential for equilibrium between masks and orchestra. The mere raising of an arm or taking a forward step becomes of extreme importance with a masked figure. It is comparable with the violinist's arm itself suggesting the sound. The fact that the actor's arms are made miniature by the immensity of the mask makes them stand out, fourfold, not in volume, but in visibility. Beyond that, costume was not necessary. We merely had to suggest it on the background of black tights, ruling out artistic drapery. For hanging, I used rather heavy materials, so that the flow of them should not confuse the body's outlines. Otherwise, my actors would not have been actors with false heads, but dwarfs with enormous ones. I did not make the mistake of *le Boeuf sur le Toit*, that error into which I dragged Dufy, but which Picasso pointed out to me. Every one of my artificial heads was of a different size and architecture. The voluminous final mask of the blind Oedipus was amplified by the white globes of the heads of his daughters and the oval motive worked into the chorus costumes.

The work took a month of preparation, then a month of realisation by the craftsmen who helped me. Laverdet handled the curtain and finished off the masks. Villat looked after the shapes. Mme. Bebko and her son managed some of the more subtle masks, such as the heads of horses and jackals and the features of Athene's bevel-square and green crest. The rest was made with whatever came to my hand (nails, old press-photographers' discarded bulbs), and the prodigious skill of Laverdet's assistants, who even before one explained it to them grasped the incomprehensible. It is important to bear in mind that the acting all took place high up and far away from one, I had to get it not merely across the footlights, but also across the whole orchestra and a full choir. The only thing that troubled me was being obliged to stand back to the stage, hence unable to do no more than shoot a glance at it. I kept myself informed by watching the audience, of which I had a marvellous view from the proscenium and which (except for the incurable stupidity of a few faces), was most impressive in its immobility.

# Description of
## the Tableaux

N

## ARRIVAL OF THE PLAGUE AT ATHENS
## ONE NIGHT

ONE sees the plague as a giant, with enormous pale green microbe head. It crosses the stage left to right before three young Thebans represented by one man with arms extended, in each hand a mask. Extreme left, an enormous realistic moon sweeps a slow muslin shadow left to right, this making the young man in the centre drop his two masks and face the plague. He goes up to the plague, falls to his knees, greets it and from the crook of one of the long red-draped arms takes a death's head, with which he covers his own face. He then moves left, when, overcome with a shaking fit, he crouches on the ground, back arched, then stretches out, prostrate and motionless. Now a second young man, leaving the moon device, comes down the steps extreme left, mounts the steps extreme right, perceives the plague, bends down, takes a death's head from the crook of the plague's black-draped left arm, and masks himself. He begins to shudder, and the curtain falls.

\*　　　\*　　　\*

## 2

### ATHENE'S GRIEF

THE curtain rises, to reveal two pale blue frames on which, facing each other, like reflections, are painted line-drawings of Pallas Athene, formed from the figures 7, 4, o and 1 and the hook of a 3. These frames are held from the outside by two men whose heads have black horse-tails. A sky-blue drop-cloth bearing an eye on it lowers crests which crown the two bearers, leaving a little free space between the two frames and the bottom of the triangle. When the drop-cloth becomes still, Athene mounts a stair in the centre of the stage which leads to behind this sort of frame or temple, where it ends in a plinth. Her features consist of a green bevel square surmounted by a green-crested helmet. In her right hand she carries a lance, in the left a green buckler with cross-shaped relief simulating the Medusa's features. The shield is surrounded by writhing snakes. A doubled-ended spiral spring indicates the eyes.

Athene leans her forehead against a lance (profile right-left) her foot on another black plinth. Finally, she turns her head, so that we see it in left-to-right profile. After this, she comes to rest, facing the audience, raises her left arm and hides her face behind the shield, when her face becomes that of the Medusa and the curtain falls.

*     *     *

3

THE ORACLES

THE curtain rises, to reveal three persons. In the centre, raised on an invisible cube, is Tiresias, in a yellow gown and black cloak. He has three heads, one facing the audience, two in profile, these horizontal on his shoulders. On his left, back to the audience, is Oedipus, on his right, similarly back to the audience, Jocasta. Oedipus's head is egg-shaped. Jocasta's head is a pure ellipse. They both turn towards the audience. Tiresias's hands, black, are raised right and left of the central mask towards his throat. First Jocasta, then Oedipus too, pull at white ribbons, which as they move away from him, left and right, they draw out of the mouths of the two profile heads of Tiresias. When they reach the extreme right and left of the stage, the ribbons finally come out of the mouths of the shades. They gather them into their hands— Oedipus in his right, Jocasta in her left. They flourish them,

N *

then put them down, Oedipus against his heart, Jocasta against her belly. Then they let the ribbons fall to the ground, and spread wide their empty hands. Tiresias resumes his former posture and the curtain falls.

\*        \*        \*

# 4

## THE SPHINX

THE curtain rises on a long, low *terracotta* wall on which are painted black zigzag lines, with white relief. To right and left, at either end of the wall, is a man with jackal head. Near the left-hand jackal one sees the Sphinx, in profile, facing the right-hand jackal. The Sphinx moves backwards. It wears its head and shoulders mask hanging down on his shoulders. Its extended arms are hidden by white pointed wings. On its left flank is fastened a bird's tail, which one realises when it raises one knee. It opens its wings, which had been dangling loose, and raises them. They vibrate, and he bears them slowly, moving to the far right of the wall, which now completely hides the actor's legs. Here the Sphinx halts, raises its left knee and shakes its wings. The curtain falls.

# 5

## THE OEDIPUS COMPLEX

THE curtain rises on a group of three actors in black tights. Two are on one knee, the other leg stretched behind them. Their black silhouettes clear against a pale blue background, they have half-moon masks. Together, the two half-moons make a full moon. Behind, on a cube, is the third actor, in a mask which consists of the pupil of an eye centred in the white skeleton of a fish. This actor, arms crossed, conceals his body with a dark blue drapery. This he lets fall.

At once, the half-moons separate and the actors who bear them move right and left. They about turn, to disclose a second profile silhouette. Returning to a position facing the audience, together with the central actor they make the gestures of drawing the figures 1, 3, 4 and 7 in the air. They are all three wearing white gloves. As the curtain falls the central figure ends up with the sign 0.

# 6

## THE THREE JOCASTAS

THE curtain rises on an empty stage, with—on the right of the centre steps—a dog formed by two actors, one standing with a jackal's head, the other bent, his arm round his partner's waist. A long black tail completes this silhouette. The third actor comes on by the central stairs, in his arms a doll representing the corpse of Jocasta (the mother). The actor sees the dog, falls back, turns round, tumbles down the stairs. Hanging, strangled by a red scarf, Jocasta (the wife) is lowered from the wings above. Her right hand is spread wide over her belly. Her foot projects below her robes. At once, the free actor reappears by the right-hand stairs, carrying a large head of Jocasta (the queen). The mouth of this head is open and from it emerges a long ribbon of red cloth. The dog begins to walk towards the left, followed by the actor carrying the head. Dog, actor and the red ribbon form a procession which passes across stage under the hanging doll, and the curtain falls.

# 7

## OEDIPUS AND HIS DAUGHTERS

THE curtain goes up to show two actors in black tights, at extreme right and left, on each slung a glazier's frame, from which dangle the masks of the choruses. By the centre stairs looms the voluminous mask of blind Oedipus. He comes forward till he is completely visible, then halts. His hands rest on the egg-shaped heads of his daughters. From each egg dangles a little frock, one pale mauve, the other pale blue. Oedipus kneels down and draws his daughters to his bosom. The choruses approach and take his daughters from him. They recede. Oedipus rises to his feet. With his left arm, he implores. The right-hand chorus comes back towards him and places one young daughter under his arm. Then Oedipus turns round and his daughter is passed from left to right hand. Now one only sees the back of Oedipus's black cloak and his hair, the red sheaves of his eyes and the egg with Antigone's pigtail. The group reaches the stairs and descends these as the curtain falls.

\*　　　\*　　　\*

One might have feared that this final scene, so bizarre and aggressive, would produce laughter, but the audience seemed paralysed by a stupor of panic. We perhaps owed this climate of silence followed at last by a tumultuous ovation to the fact that in stylised presentation I had gone the whole hog, though of course the presence of Stravinsky conducting the orchestra added to the general jubilation. One can hardly be angry with the press men who saw nothing but grimace and caricature, when one recalls that even Charles Maurras says the primitive heads of the Acropolis museum are merely "scarecrow things".

The back drop was an enormous painted canvas (with greys, mauves, beiges and sulphurous yellow predominating) inspired by one of my drawings for la Machine Infernale. Blind Oedipus and Jocasta, with distorted shapes, loomed from the rungs of this.

# On a Trip to Greece

> The traveller fell dead, struck by the picturesqueness.
>
> *Max Jacob.*

IT needs saying with resolution, the fact seeming so bizarre: Greece is a notion which one forms and which continues incessantly to form under a sky which is absolutely made for such fantasies even to the point of wonder whether Greece really exists, whether indeed one is oneself when one travels there and if all its isles and that Athens where the pepper-mills stricken the air with their dust are not mere fabulous things, a presence equally as strong and equally as dead as those, for instance, of Pallas Athene or Neptune. One wonders. Clambering goatlike over the bones of kings embalmed by those everlasting flowers from which the storm draws a brew of odours as vital and as defunct as that Waggoner who without stirring a foot strides on ever, traversing the ages, eyes groping forward like the white staff of the blind. A notion made and a notion for ever unmade, mortal and everlasting like these same dry blooms which rustle in the sun about the grotto where the sybil prophesied, the door where her Sunday clients queued. Yes, a notion, a fixed notion, so fixed that on its oracular legs it stands stock-still staring at us with unseeing eye. And that eye of the notion opens everywhere, at Delphi, with the crown of its sometime stage, and on Crete, when we feared to get lost in the open labyrinth of Knossos where lurk the notions of red bull and bees, as witness the skep-like hills and the waists of princes and princesses, laced mercilessly into the walls and the columns of blood. And that Isle of Santorin which escapes its volcanoes solely by its white flight to the summit of the lava peaks. And that notion, that notion browsed by the sea whispering it to itself till time without end and a man shall sacrifice his daughter so that it shall be stilled and its nagging murmur not rock this boat which is mere notion of boat, floating better than on any sea on these flowing waters where heroes are but their own shades. And in this notion of a place infernal, these other notions of men and women join in marriage and copulate and engender till with their progeny they fill all the world of memories. There you have indeed a notion, a crazy man's notion, one of those notions which medical science treats in closed clinic gardens packed with travellers like ourselves. There you have that Greece elusive, where by which crevice or cave one never knows, one penetrates to seek that dog Cerberus by his master lost, which Heracles must ferret out for him, stealing oranges, wielding his broom for Augeas, and at Lerna draining swamps for all this to turn to hound with triple head, to hydra, to rivers diverted, to apples of gold, and one believes in it all because the lips which murmur such tales never lie but charge History with falsity, History being never notion, merely a procession of defunct deeds which clutter the boards of a stage. This notion we are compelled to admit because we found we were in it, ourselves notion, one flesh with the notion which contained us and at the same time became our substance. How indeed emerge therefrom without, like Ulysses glued to his seat, leaving behind us a part of our person? That seemed out of the question, the winds veering and opposing our flight. What am I saying? It was notions of wind like those young sons of Boreas who could no longer stand Heracles' hunting stories and dumped him marooned on an islet, where he cried out to his young pal in a voice which the nymphs could not bear, so, stopping their ears, came to drown him. Another notion which became that of Ulysses, further astonishing the notion of the sirens' song. For the great gods a question mark and how from that cycle escape and will not the angel appear which shall sound the loud blast of the trumpet and its notion of trumpet shall be our dream and twist round the poles as it did at King Ajax's funeral, then, wiping its lips, disappeared? For that angel was a notion to which disappearance was proper once another came on its heels and with reason since the notion which pursued it was that of a cataclysm which the Bible records and that Saint John had the notion of eating in book form on the Island of Patmos where we had no notion of going, so much was the notion of it in the air.

In the Ionian Sea one has no notion of travel and if one has, the only way of getting out of it is again a notion, an eagle notion, coming from Zeus's own notion of his powers, excusing the notion Xerxes had of flogging the ocean, or Caesar of outraging a river, or the Thracians of launching their arrows against the sky. Take refuge in a museum? What was the use? For there, we should be lost among the trees of the forest of the victims of the Gorgon Medusa, and the broken branches of those trees would find the means of stringing us up with notions of hands as we passed. Ah, it is frightful, though many a tourist never grasps a bit of it, by his lack of notions miraculously withstanding the notion which in him stifles all notions. Of this we took stock at the theatre of Dinoysos whose erotic notions did not contaminate a single one of the females we saw visiting them under guidely protection against any notion and clad in macks guaranteed to let not even a dewdrop through. The mere fear of being Medusaed by that sequence of notions, by that dangerous buckler she wielded, put us on our guard and we were wary, and I still am, and after a long night of that sleep which massacres a man and spares but his notions, I am still haunted by the notion of Greece.